EXPERT WITNESS

Testimony of a Former 4ᵗʰ Generation Jehovah's Witness

GAIL THERESA WHITE

Expert Witness: Testimony of a Former 4th Generation Jehovah's Witness.

ISBN 978-1-7341328-0-9 (paperback)

ISBN 978-1-7341328-1-6 (ebook)

ISBN 978-1-7341328-2-3 (audio book)

Library of Congress Cataloging-in-Publication Data: An application to register this book for cataloging has been submitted to the Library of Congress.

Cover design by: Melvin McClanahan

Photographs by: Joe R. O'Bryant, Jr.

Printed in the United States of America

CONNECT WITH GAIL

https://www.GailTheresaWhite.com

OR

@GailTheresaWhite on:

DEDICATION

This book is dedicated to my one and only Sophia. I am so blessed to call you my daughter. We have a special bond that others will never understand. I promised God I would take good care of you and I thank Him every day for choosing me to be your mother.

To Susan, woman of God, thank you for accepting me as I am and creating a safe environment for me to express myself freely. May God continue to bless you, your family, and your life-saving work.

Finally, thank you to my Heavenly Father for keeping me safe and protected during my time in the wilderness and for honoring your Word. I give you all the glory, honor, and praise. Amen!

"You are my witnesses," declares the L ORD,
"and my servant whom I have chosen,
so that you may know and believe me
and understand that I am he.
Before me no god was formed,
nor will there be one after me."

Isaiah 43:10

TABLE OF CONTENTS

ACKNOWLEDGEMENTS

I would like to thank my parents, first and foremost, for successfully raising seven children with a spiritual mindset. As I said in my letter, your efforts did not go unnoticed and I appreciate all the sacrifices you both made to inculcate God into our minds and hearts. You did not fail me, and I love you both unconditionally.

To my brother, Peter White, how brave you were for having gone through this. Thank you for not giving up on yourself all those years ago and taking a stand. I am proud of the man you have become. Thank you also for your financial contribution toward publishing this book and believing in this labor of love. Love you bro!

Thank you, Chris, for your motivational support. Receiving those inspirational messages every morning kept me going and gave me the push I needed in those final weeks. One Love!

To my incredible editor, Jill, thank you for your professionalism and guidance throughout this entire process. You are a true gem and I consider you my friend.

To my Second family, thank you for your kindness and support. Although you may not understand fully *the other gospel* and sometimes may not always know what to say; know that a simple hello, your friendly smiles and hugs have made all the difference in the world. They opened me up to the amazement that exists outside of the only life I had ever known.

i

And finally, to my fellow Expert Witnesses, thank you for speaking up, giving your testimonies, sharing your heartbreaking stories, and taking a firm stand. Your courage and dedication were an instrumental part of my healing process and confirmed that I was not crazy. Together we are making a difference. Let's keep telling the truth, defending those who have not yet found their voice, and continue to be inspired by the ones who tragically gave up—may it never happen to another. We are about to breakthrough. Somebody is waiting for us to show up. Let your voices be heard.

!!!

INTRODUCTION | EXPERT WITNESS

Hi, my name is Gail White, and I was a 4th generation Jehovah's Witness. Internally, the members refer to it as "the truth." I woke up to the deception and was faced with an agonizing decision. Deciding I could no longer be a part of the organization came at a hefty cost; my family and friends I had made over my lifetime.

You may wonder why even write this book. Why not leave well enough alone? I got out and now I've moved on. I get it; however, it is not quite as easy as it may seem. My fifty-year involvement with this organization sets me up with a unique perspective and insights I can now use to bring awareness to the system that envelopes a Jehovah's Witnesses life and existence. Because of this, I am reaching out to as many people as I can—whether through this book, on social media, podcasts, etc.

The parent company of Jehovah's Witnesses is the Watchtower Bible and Tract Society. The Watchtower began publishing in 1879. In 1884, Charles Taze Russell and a small group established the International Bible Students to separate themselves from Christendom's clergy and is a branch out from the Adventist movement of William Miller. The Bible Students officially adopted the name, Jehovah's Witnesses in 1931 and on JW.org, the organization now writes that Jesus was essentially its founder.

This is an organization with a worldwide presence, having a lot of power to influence many generations through its expectations of how a witness should act, believe, and even think. To give you an idea...when my family relocated to

America in the summer of 1978, we easily found a kingdom hall just a few blocks from our new home. We didn't skip a beat.

We used the same books as we did back in Jamaica and picked up right where we left off. In my 10-year old mind, this was proof I was in the true religion. If I could travel to 240+ countries, walk into a kingdom hall, and study the same exact Watchtower I would if I were home, that represented something legitimate.

In addition, winter came quickly after our move, and we were not adequately prepared. The friends heard about our dilemma, got together, and set us up with clothes and boots for the winter. We left every meeting with bags of clothes. We were overwhelmed with the kindness shown to us. What other religion was that loving, unified, and organized? We felt very fortunate.

I had experienced their kindness as an adult, as well. As a young single mom, trying to raise my daughter, God had guided a great blessing toward us, and I give Him the glory for it to this day. In order to get my daughter and I into a home—the home I still own today—a brother and his family gifted me the required 10% down payment. I was so grateful for that, then and now.

JW's are not bad people and most of them are very kind. But many are unknowing participants in a system that can be swift, cruel, and unjust.

Conversely, when one is disfellowshipped or excommunicated, there is no such thing as moving to another congregation and starting over. You will be shunned by all of Jehovah's Witnesses, all over the world. Records are kept of field service hours, shepherding calls, and disciplinary actions.

Watchtower may not be the only organization that leads its members this way. However, it is the only one I am qualified to discuss because it had been my entire life as a 4th generation, up until the fall of 2017. I had lived my entire life in a lie. What scares me most is I was working with a fervor to make my daughter the 5th generation of witnesses in my family lineage. Having multiple generations in this organization is viewed as having a rich spiritual heritage, and this surely came with much pressure.

As a witness, we learned how to overcome objections to our beliefs. A common one was that Jehovah's Witnesses had their own Bible, but they never substantiated what they meant. Or they would say that we did not believe in Jesus. When I showed them from the Bible that we did, they were stumped. I was baffled and didn't understand where they got that incorrect information. Today, I understand what they were trying to say and why they thought that way. This book will help you to continue the conversation.

In this book, I also contrast and compare, as well as to go back to the beginning, as far as the language is concerned. Therefore, I reference the Greek Interlinear extensively, as well as many of the most popular Bible versions, including the New International Version (NIV).

These resources, along with the internet, have shown me what is translated in the New World Translation of the Holy Scriptures (NWT), does not align.

With you, I share insights regarding how and why this exists. What has happened is not my story alone. The same things have happened to countless others. Some have shared their stories, some stories are yet to be revealed, and others could not bear the harsh reality of ostracism and sadly resorted to taking their lives. These children of God were so worn down; no longer able to fight for themselves. Their stories cannot be lost.

All these stories are important and deserve to be heard.

I welcome you to gain a better understanding of what happens in the world of Jehovah's Witnesses from the perspective of an Expert Witness.

1

PART I | CRUEL & UNUSUAL PUNISHMENT

1 | THE TRIAL AND THE VERDICT

Do not judge, or you too will be judged. For in the same way you judge others, you will be judged, and with the measure you use, it will be measured to you.

Matthew 7:1-2

It had been a bad idea to invite the elders to my home. I felt cornered, trapped. It had taken me some time to muster up the courage to even make the call, but I prayed and asked Jehovah for the strength to do it. This type of visit was called a "shepherding call." During this type of call, the brothers come to share encouraging scriptures and to build you up spiritually. The reason for my request was I had been inactive for quite some time and wanted to take the steps to get back into my spiritual routine. This meant clearing my conscience first.

Now that they were there before me, I had a problem. I didn't have the courage to tell them why I had really called them to my home. It was not the first time I had to go before the brothers to confess a sin. In fact, it was my fourth.

On two occasions, I was privately reproved for what I shared with them. This means they had found me to be sufficiently repentant, readjusted me privately, and there was no formal announcement made to the congregation.

One other time I was publicly reproved, which means a public announcement was made during a meeting that I had been reproved. These actions, which are decided by a committee of three elders, are considered forms of discipline to "instill wholesome fear in the onlookers" and to "keep the congregation clean." Some privileges such as commenting and giving talks may be restricted, but meeting attendance and field service are still expected. These disciplinary actions do not result in shunning. However, people are aware there is an issue and may or may not limit their association with you.

By the way, the embarrassment of these moments rarely leaves, not entirely, anyway.

As bad as either a public or private reproving sounds, there is another form of discipline that is feared, dreaded by most JW's because of the repercussions that follow. Disfellowshipping! Being disfellowshipped means all JW's cannot speak to you. This includes your family and friends. They will not acknowledge your existence, not a hello, not a nod, not even a smile. You become a stranger and are treated as if you are dead.

Now, there I was this day, a fourth-time offender. A repeat offender. I had no idea what to expect but only knew it would be nerve-racking and humiliating, as confessions always are. However, in my mind and heart, if that was the price I had to pay to get right with Jehovah, I would do it. For my daughter, if no one else. I wanted to get our family back into the spiritual routine of serving Jehovah together. She had grown disinterested in going to the meetings. This made me feel inadequate as a parent; especially knowing I had let both her and Jehovah down. Finding the courage to do whatever it took to right the wrong, even if it meant the dreaded disfellowshipping, had to be done. So be it.

The constant thought of Armageddon being right around the corner was another motivating factor for me to get my relationship right with Jehovah. What if Armageddon came the next day? I wanted nothing more than to have everlasting life and be in paradise with my daughter. To ensure we would be there, I needed the help of the brothers to guide me through this current situation.

This day, it did not work.

After they left, I was still feeling convicted.

So, I made the agonizing decision to schedule another shepherding call.

It was time to clear my conscience once and for all and move on with our lives. Setting a good example for Sophia mattered greatly. She knew what I had done to get into the situation in the first place. It was paramount to get her into paradise right along with me. She has such a fervent love for animals, and she would want to be there; I knew that's where she belonged.

At the next meeting, I told one of the brothers I needed to talk with them again. However, Hurricane Harvey hit the area and "as soon as possible" turned into a couple of months. After all the chaos and cleanup work, the two elders came back to my home. Finally, the time had arrived for me to come clean.

After some small talk about the terrible flooding in our area, I got right into it. Saying what I needed to confess in front of a group of men was not easy. It involved revealing intimate details many women might not share with anyone else. It would be impossible for most people to go to the meetings and not feel riddled with guilt, especially when immorality was the topic of discussion.

I explained why I had called them back and the conversation turned serious. They asked a few questions to determine if a judicial committee would need to be formed. They told me they would get back with me as soon as possible.

This time around, there was no delay. They were swift in getting back with me. In less than a week, the judicial committee was formed, and the date and time were now set.

What is a judicial committee? A judicial committee consists of at least three elders in the congregation. Elders are appointed men who are entrusted with the responsibility of leading "the sheep." At times, this may include administering discipline, should it become necessary. Elders are appointed by the Holy Spirit.

During my time as a witness, I had come to trust the brothers and really believed they were there to "be a refuge from the rainstorm," "shepherds of the flock."

Articles from The Watchtower encouraged us to seek the help of the elders. "Always Accept Jehovah's Discipline" is one these articles and this excerpt is dated November 15, 2006 and is from paragraphs 17-18.

> **17.** Why should we not hesitate to seek the spiritual help of the elders?
>
> [17] The elders gladly comply with this counsel: "Continue showing mercy. . . , doing so with fear." (Jude 23) By falling into sexual immorality, some

Christians have sinned seriously. But if they are truly repentant, they can expect merciful, loving treatment by elders eager to help them spiritually. Including himself, Paul said regarding such men: "Not that we are the masters over your faith, but we are fellow workers for your joy." (2 Corinthians 1:24) Therefore, never hesitate to seek their spiritual assistance.

18. How do elders deal with erring fellow believers?

[18] If you have sinned seriously, why can you have confidence in the elders? Because they are primarily shepherds of God's flock. (1 Peter 5:1-4) No loving shepherd beats a docile, bleating lamb for hurting itself. When elders deal with erring fellow believers, therefore, it is a matter, not of crime and punishment, but of sin and spiritual restoration where possible. (James 5:13-20) Elders must judge with righteousness and "treat the flock with tenderness." (Acts 20:29, 30; Isaiah 32:1, 2) Like all other Christians, elders are to 'exercise justice, love kindness, and be modest in walking with God.' (Micah 6:8) Such qualities are vital when making decisions involving the life and sacred service of "the sheep of [Jehovah's] pasturage."—Psalm 100:3.

Most everything JWs study is in a question and answer format. Also, with the teachings of JW, it is easy to develop the trait of guilt.

Here is another example, taken from the article, "Are You Taking Refuge in Jehovah?" This was in the November 2017 Watchtower, paragraph 8.

> "…a Christian guilty of serious sin needs to seek the help of congregation elders to recover… elders are commissioned and trained to reassure repentant sinners, helping to ease their pain and guilt. Jehovah calls these older men "a refuge from the rainstorm." (Isaiah 32:1, 2, ftn.) Would you not agree that this arrangement is an expression of God's mercy?"

I would later find out that elders are given a book, published by Watchtower, called *Shepherd the Flock of God.* Most of Jehovah's Witnesses are unaware of this book's existence. The following excerpt is taken from that book, under the section, "Preparing Your Mind and Heart to Judge." This entire book, which anyone can now find through a simple internet search, is quite disturbing and reveals just how legalistic this organization is.

Preparing Your Mind and Heart to Judge

3. Serving on a judicial committee is a heavy responsibility. You are judging for Jehovah and are accountable to him for the judgment you render. (2 Chron. 19:6, 7) Your decision will likely have long-lasting and far-reaching consequences for the individual involved, his Christian family members, and others in the congregation. *Each time* **you serve on a judicial committee, you should first review Chapters 5-7 of this publication.**

4. Allowing an unrepentant wrongdoer to remain in the congregation could result in a leavening influence. (Gal. 5:9) Failure to remove the individual may also minimize the wrong in the mind of the wrongdoer and in the minds of others who may know of his sin. (Eccl. 8:11) On the other hand, an individual unjustly dealt with may have difficulty recovering his spirituality.—Matt. 18:6.

5. You can render a good judgment with Jehovah's help. (Matt. 18:18-20) Pray for wisdom, discernment, and God's holy spirit. (1 Ki. 3:9; Phil. 1:9, 10; Jas. 1:5) Do careful, thorough research using Bible-based publications, not relying solely on past experience in handling judicial matters. (Prov. 15:28) Endeavor to obtain a clear picture regarding what occurred and what the individual's true attitude is. —Prov. 18:13, 17.

NOTE: Within the text above, Holy Spirit is in lower case. I am intrigued by this. Could the text be an oversight or typographical error? Nevertheless, when it comes to spiritual matters, does Jehovah really call on man to judge another man?

Appearing before the Judicial Committee

I was ready to face any consequence, be it public reproof or disfellowshipping. (Or so I told myself.)

Only a handful of days passed since the brothers visited my home that second time. Now it was Tuesday night, 7:00 PM, and I was already at the kingdom hall waiting for the official judicial committee meeting to start.

This was terrifying, but I was repentant and wanted a fresh start. So...

The three brothers who made up the committee I was being judged by sat right across from me, in very close proximity. One about three feet away, the other slightly more. As we waited for the third brother to show up, they tried to lighten the atmosphere with small talk. They were quite jovial and appeared calm as they spoke among themselves. They may have felt at ease, but I remained terrified. I was ready to get this over with.

These three brothers consisted of one who was on my last committee 10 years ago; the second, was a long-time acquaintance from the same country as my family; and a third, whom I had recently met and who worked with my brother.

The meeting began and the time started to pass by. This is what took place for the next 5 1/2 hours...

They started with a word of prayer. Prayer is important because this is how elders lead the hearing to ensure they are being led by the Holy Spirit. What really stood out to me about this prayer is how they kept stressing for me to be honest and forthright; to tell the truth and not hold anything back. Did they forget I had brought up my situation to them? They didn't bust me doing anything; I turned myself in. Why would I now lie or hold anything back?

I had always been a "by the book" type of person. Even though I had transgressed, I was now going by the book and came forward on my own volition. You can imagine how awkward this was, but I was so compelled to come clean that it left me no other choice.

They established how everything about to take place would be confidential, aside from their decision. This would be shared with the body of elders, should there be a need for an announcement. I was relieved. After all, I was about to share very personal, highly sensitive, and embarrassing information.

They also had notebooks which I thought nothing of at the time. All three assured me they were just jotting down notes, which would be destroyed immediately following the meeting that night. I felt a sense of relief and more at ease. I trusted them completely.

Quite quickly, my trust wavered. The atmosphere had changed, the tone had changed, and things began to get intense.

Let me pause here and share this. Some might find it unnerving that this type of committee is made up entirely of men; that I am by myself, with no one for moral support. But because of the trust factor and being a lifelong JW, this was not an issue for me. That's just the way it was and the way it had always been.

In past meetings, they would ask a variety of intrusive and personal questions. Questions such as: How much contact did you have? Was there fondling? Was there penetration? What kind of sex? How many times? When? Where? Did you not think about Jehovah? And on and on.

This time, however, there was only one question. How many times? Once. Twice. More than a dozen. I finally answered yes, it was more than a dozen times.

After admitting this, the brother who had been doing most of the questioning at that point sat back in his chair and had such a distinct expression on his face as he glanced over at the others. We were only 15 minutes in, and I could tell his mind was already made up. This was a done deal, I thought, and my heart sank.

Yet, I admitted my wrongdoing, while also stating my intention. *"I choose Jehovah and I want to do what's pleasing to Him."*

I felt alone. Like no other JW had struggled with any part of their relationship with Jehovah the way I did. Did I not have Jehovah's favor? Was I not spiritual enough? Had I not been forgiven for my past sins; the other times I had sat in front of a committee?

These are the thoughts that linger in the mind of a JW when faced with challenges. Instead of realizing life has its ups and downs, a JW will view it as a punishment or believe they are not doing enough for Jehovah. For instance:

I had been pouring out my heart out to a friend about some things involving work, relationships in my life, and a few trying events. She found it hard to believe I could go through all the stuff I was going through and not go crazy. Then she asked the question which perfectly shows the JW mindset: "Are you sure you're not hiding something?" Her straightforward question said it all. My hardships were happening because I was involved in wrongdoing. At that time, I was not.

A family member also said a similar thing a few years prior. He was surprised I had not been remarried and was even curious about how it was possible for me to go so long without sex. There are no boundaries, and some feel they have the right to police you. He too asked if I needed to go to the brothers to confess something. The presumption was I must be hiding a secret sin and thus not getting my blessing from Jehovah.

The inference was that a hidden transgression was a direct link to why I struggled.

Obviously…

A failed marriage.

A foreclosed house.

A repossessed car.

A single mom since age twenty-five.

Challenges at work.

These were the only two people who had the boldness to say what they did to me.

How many others were thinking the same thing and just kept it to themselves?

These assumptions are not comforting to a single JW woman. Of course, I had developed a complex and it only validated my insecurity that *something was wrong with me*.

Where was my mate? I had, like other single JW women do, kept going with a determination to put Jehovah first.

Life becomes a state of self-condemnation. In the moment of interrogation, despite my condemning thoughts putting me on a mental trial, I continued answering the questions asked of me by the elders.

And keep in mind, I only knew people in the JW organization.

For me, life was fast paced. I was constantly on the go and I always rushed to get to meetings. In the early years, work usually took me downtown, with an hour commute each way. But my last years as a witness, was spent working in the family business; working 60-70+ hours each week.

Being a single mother was not always easy. Despite being blessed to work much closer to home, my daughter was what I cherished coming home to. This remained true even when all else was falling apart.

Rest and sleep were precious commodities I was lacking in.

Because of the struggles despite my fight to remain faithful, I knew one thing: If Jehovah was going to bless me, He would have done it by now. Anything lacking only showed His displeasure for me.

My thoughts were this dark and ugly.

When I wasn't tough on myself, other peoples' words affirmed what I was already thinking. Human decency had been abandoned, and wrong motives were impugned toward me, at least from my perspective.

I'd been pushing so long and there was nothing left in the tank. Life had become weary and burdensome.

It had been a while since I had gone in field service, which is the work of knocking on doors, and had missed a lot of meetings. This was a problem and indicated the reason why I fell into sin.

When a person becomes inactive, they are perceived as being spiritually weak, thereby having a strained relationship with Jehovah.

One of the elders commented on this and then brought up my meeting attendance or lack thereof. I had only been making a few each month, compared to two a week plus field service.

At this point in the meeting, the elder I'd recently met made the comment that if I had been regular in all these activities, we wouldn't be sitting here, now would we?

The condescending look he had on his face left me feeling completely unsettled.

No comfort offered, no empathy detected, no mercy or compassion for the years of trying to be a good JW. I certainly wasn't feeling the love.

I'm thinking, *how do these people know my relationship with God?* They are clearly basing my relationship with God by what I do or don't do.

Being labeled "inactive" was so offensive to me because I had a personal relationship with God despite the chaos of my life. It just wasn't their idea of what it should look like. I had never liked hearing that expression applied to others nor did I feel it was my place to judge another person's standing before Jehovah based on their meeting attendance and field service activity. Who are any of us to define what someone's relationship or spiritual connection with God is like?

In any case, I never thought the label of being "inactive" would one day apply to me. Although inactive, I still prayed to Jehovah and felt my prayers were being heard. Even though in my mind I had rejected the label, I knew how others were trained to view me. I wasn't following their routine, which meant I was headed in the wrong direction.

I didn't respond. I wouldn't have been sitting there if I hadn't gone to them. Making a response would have only sounded like I was trying to justify or minimize my behavior and the dilemma I now found myself in.

In a nutshell, inconsistent meeting attendance and no field service time equates to a poor relationship with Jehovah.

This is the judgmental atmosphere that persists.

Questions became even more intense and to protect others privacy, I will withhold those here. However, what I revealed should have been alarming enough for any normal, blood running through their veins, human being to feel some sort of empathy.

They basically dismissed what I shared and said they were not here to talk about that, only this situation.

Circumstances were irrelevant.

Instead, the message was how I had brought all this on myself by not following the guidelines of the organization.

There was no excuse or justifiable reason for falling into sin...again, if I really loved Jehovah and his commandments. There was no room for error. Perfection was expected. If others could do it successfully, so could I.

"I'm so tired, I just feel like giving up." As hard as it was to say, either they didn't know what I meant, or they didn't care. This was an entirely true statement, but it was overlooked by their eagerness to handle my current situation.

It was a "hmm" moment. Was I justifying it?

Time moved slowly and I continued to pour out my heart. My actions were supposed to be the right thing; an opportunity to show remorse and awareness of the situation.

Elders were elevated as individuals who cared for the flock, but I was looking at three people who were not interested in considering any role other than that of a disciplinarian.

Zero humanity! This really came to light in what happened next.

First, a bit of background. Prior to the meeting, I had been seeing a therapist because of other issues and stressful events I had been experiencing.

During the meeting, I mentioned I had been going to therapy to help me cope. One of the brothers seemed shocked and asked about it.

He asked: "How long have you been seeing the therapist?"

"A year and a half," I replied.

"And you're just now coming to us? Don't you think you should have come to us first?"

I was visibly startled and taken back by the question. I didn't answer. He had a look of disapproval on his face and glanced over at the other two as he relaxed back into his chair.

They also brought up the amount of time it took for me to confess and it clearly worked against me. My apprehension, the length of time involved in the sin, and the delay from the hurricane were now being used against me.

Although forgiveness comes from Jehovah, confessing my sins in prayer to God was only the first step. A witness goes one step further and confesses to the elders, who then pray on the witness's behalf. The implication for me in this situation was that my relationship with Him was damaged and I needed their help to mend it. Apparently, my praying directly to God was not enough.

Can you believe this? I can, because I lived it, not knowing any better for a good portion of my life.

Yet, I kept saying: "I choose Jehovah." And I meant it.

In my heart, I felt God had forgiven me. But the process was more complicated than what my heart felt. There was the information in the JW publications to take into consideration.

Every talk, every article, every piece of literature exhorts a member to one solution: If you have erred, to get your life on track, you must go to the elders.

The evening kept getting more bizarre, my thoughts clearer. It was much easier to confess and talk to God, rather than these men.

At that moment I understood and can now relate to what Job meant when he said:

> But I desire to speak to the Almighty and to argue my case with God. You, however, smear me with lies; you are worthless physicians, all of you!
>
> Job 13:3-4

It all sounds so logical now from my current perspective; however, at the time it seemed logical. It all tripped me up because of the contradictions. Furthermore, there was no room to express any opinion contrary to the articles and what they expressed one should believe or how they should act.

Finally, the meeting got to a point where they asked me to leave the room.

I got up, went to take a seat in the auditorium, and waited.

This is the part where they deliberated, and I would find out my fate.

Minutes turned into an hour before I was finally called back into the room.

There was no decision. Instead, there were more questions. They were confused and needed some more clarification, which I offered. I suspect they were also reviewing past information from the previous decade, if not more. They were not supposed to have information like that saved according to their own words, but apparently, they did. One of the elders had been on the committee that had privately reproved me ten years ago. Did he remember my details from back then? It seemed likely.

I answered the same questions again and poured out my heart again.

They read scriptures to me and something out the book, *Insight on the Scriptures*, published by Watchtower, which is like an encyclopedia or commentary for JWs. It was something like: "the degree of discipline being commensurate with the degree of wrongdoing." Later, I found out the quote was not as it was read to me, an embellishment to serve their purposes, whatever said purposes were. More accurately, it was the degree of one's repentance that should be commensurate to the degree of the sin.

They began to use word problems to make their point.

"If you were driving down the road and you pass the stop sign and you went a mile away from where you should have turned, how long would it take you to get back to where you should have turned?"

"A mile."

"Alright then." Was that a hint as to how long it was going to take me to make my way back? I had veered so far off course that it would take so long to make the situation right.

Again, I was asked to leave the room.

Now I was beyond worried, as I realized where I was probably headed; the worst-case scenario. *I was being disfellowshipped.*

I took note of the clock and saw it was past my usual early bedtime. This time around, they deliberated even longer, more than an hour. This was so serious.

At 12:10 AM, I was called back into the room.

The Verdict

They started by commending me for coming forward because in their words, "many never do." There are those who keep the information to themselves and never get the spiritual help they need…

As they went on, I felt a glimmer of hope!

Then it turned cold again. My behavior showed a pattern of wrongdoing and previous disciplinary actions did not prove helpful.

"The decision is to disfellowship."

The word "disfellowship" jolted me like a bolt of lightning that went from the top of my head straight through my heart and I saw a flash of white light. I was devastated!

From that point on, their words faded away as I struggled to recover from the shock.

"We can't read hearts," they said. They couldn't tell if I was repentant. What did they mean, they couldn't tell? JW's are taught these meetings are guided by the Holy Spirit, inspired by God. So why were these men trying to read my heart and why weren't my words enough?

They continued, telling me that they need to see proof of my repentance. They called it "works befitting repentance."

Seriously?

Proof? What about Jehovah? I had believed this was about showing my repentance to Jehovah. Where was He in all of this?

Continuing to come to the kingdom hall to attend meetings where no one would greet or speak to me would prove my repentance.

My heartfelt words had not been enough for these men. Now, I must prove my sincerity. What had I just spent the past five hours doing? I'd poured out my heart and willingly put myself through the entire process.

In a state of shock, I softly spoke: "I thought disfellowshipping was for those who were unrepentant." It was just a whisper, but they heard me.

As his face turned red, one of the elders repeated the stop sign scenario to me slowly as if I weren't getting it; as if they were speaking to a child, talking down to me, with an element of authority.

They resumed what they considered to be a loving tone, explaining why this decision was made.

They read one last scripture to me from Hebrews 12:6 (NWT):

> …for those whom Jehovah loves he disciplines, in fact, he scourges everyone whom he receives as a son. (NWT)

"Jehovah loves you and we care about you too." Love? This is what you call love? I had never felt so unloved.

"We're doing this to save your life." They reminded me the end is coming soon, and I didn't want Armageddon to come with me in a disfellowshipped state; and I must work as hard as I could and come back to Jehovah quickly.

They concluded by informing me about the seven-day window and my right to appeal.

How should I have responded? I do not know. I was in shock and disbelief. But I was too ashamed, emotionally and physically exhausted, to plea my case any further. I made up my mind to humbly accept the discipline as God's arrangement of dealing with me. After all, He is Holy, and He expects us to be Holy.

"You're dismissed," one elder said.

That was it. I was dismissed without even so much as a prayer or a handshake, and…

…at 12:15 AM, the verdict was in.

2 | APPEAL AND RESCIND

Have pity on me, my friends, have pity, for the hand of God has struck me.

Job 19:21

The drive home that night was strange, replaying what had happened over the past five hours, how late it was, and how tricked I felt. Tricked into coming forward, tricked into oversharing. It was also highly inappropriate for me to be on the road so late, unaccompanied although on my way home.

By morning, the thought that the judicial committee possibly had notes on me from previous situations over the past thirty-plus years disturbed me. I couldn't shake it. They had implicitly stated these types of notes and files were just for the specific day in mind, not some running record of me as a person—as a JW.

I called Watchtower headquarters to request a copy of my file. I was transferred to someone in the service department who tried to figure out the purpose of my request. He asked: "Are you about to be disciplined?" I don't mind saying I wish I would have lied and said "no." I was truthful and said "yes." He responded that they don't have any files and quickly ended the conversation.

I did get to the task of thinking about what I would have to do to appeal the decision.

A few days later, my dad came to pick me up for a business appointment.

I shared with him that I had to go to the brothers and that the decision was to disfellowship, but I was going to appeal. I told him something didn't feel right. I had experienced no mercy, no love, no compassion. It had almost felt personal.

He didn't have much to say. Only mentioning things like "I don't know what to say" or "just hurry up and come back."

How can you hurry and come back when they are the ones in total control of determining how long you are disfellowshipped?

I asked if he could help me write the appeal letter. To which he answered "no." I had known what he was going to say. Why did I even bother?

Loyalty to Jehovah comes first. Any decision the brothers make is accepted without question. Questioning would show a lack of humility and a haughty spirit.

We were often told to "wait on Jehovah" who straightens matters out and makes injustices right, in time.

I felt helpless in many ways but inside of me, I was compelled to do what I felt was right. They may have thought the decision was in, but I wasn't going to be set up in the light they would paint of me.

The process of figuring out an effective appeal was my biggest priority. My case would be heard, no matter how many obstacles I faced. I didn't want to lose everybody I was close to.

The first step was to notify them of my plan to appeal.

I had one more day within the seven-day window to appeal and finally sent an email of my intent to appeal. I waited until the eleventh hour, which happened to fall on a meeting night.

However, after researching the Watchtower publication *Organized to Accomplish God's Ministry*, I realized an appeal entails going before a new committee of three different elders. There was no way I was going to put myself through that ordeal again. So, I decided to drop it.

The appeal window expired.

I went to the meeting the next evening, the evening of the announcement. Knowing the announcement was forthcoming, I texted my family members to tell them there would be an announcement.

One of my regrets was I included my mom in the text, instead of calling her. The reason for my impersonal delivery of the message was I did not want to talk to anyone about it. I needed a reprieve from the draining process I'd gone through. My mindset: Let's get this over with.

Here are some of the responses to my text:

- We look forward to talking to you as soon as you get back.
- Thanks for letting me know. Other servants in Bible times and present have been disciplined by Jehovah and made a speedy recovery. I know this will be so in your case. I love you.

This is what the conversation would have been had I called them. I was not interested in hearing it. The overall sentiment was they were glad I had taken the steps laid out by the organization; that I was on the right path of becoming reconciled with Jehovah and hoped I would be reinstated before Armageddon came.

There was only one phone call my daughter encouraged me to make. It was to a sister who was like a second mom to me. We had become friends after Hurricane Katrina more than a decade earlier. We rode together to conventions and the meetings she attended in person. Otherwise, there was the option to listen in on the telephone line.

I knew she would be listening in that night and didn't want to catch her off guard. Thinking of her hearing the news over the phone didn't feel right. So before walking into the kingdom hall, I made the phone call.

I told her there was going to be an announcement that night.

She said: "What announcement, baby?"

"An announcement about me." She still didn't understand what I meant. I finally told her I was going to be read out that night and she went into a panic.

"Oh no, oh no, oh my God."

She asked me if the brothers had been working with me and I was just not responding to their counsel?

The reason she asked me such a question at that time was because their publications lead the witnesses to believe they have worked with the person and have reasoned with them and they just refuse to change their sinful ways and are unrepentant. Therefore, disfellowshipping is justified. Here is another example of what is taught to every single witness:

Watchtower (Study Edition), "Why Disfellowshipping is a Loving Provision," April 15, 2015, pp. 29-31.

Two factors—which must coincide—result in the disfellowshipping of one of Jehovah's Witnesses. First, a baptized Witness commits a serious sin. Second, he does not repent of his sin.

God pardoned David's sin because of David's sincere repentance. (Ps. 32:1-5) Likewise, a servant of Jehovah today will be disfellowshipped only if he is unrepentant or continues to practice what is bad. (Acts 3:19; 26:20) If genuine repentance is not manifest to the elders who serve on a judicial committee, they must disfellowship the person.

I told her: "No, my last meeting was ten years ago."

Finally, she understood and said with some sadness and the expected sentiments, to hurry up and come back before the end comes.

We said our goodbyes and that was our last conversation.

I'm not going to lie. I have had those same sentiments toward family and close friends who were disfellowshipped in the past.

You literally hold your breath, hoping they will come back before the end comes. I can't believe I used to think and live in such fear. I feel such a sense of relief; like a boulder has been lifted from the burden of such horrifying thoughts.

It was October 2017 and I entered the hall a few minutes early. The announcement of my disfellowshipping would be made soon. Was I ready to hear it in front of all these people? No, not really.

People were speaking to me and making small talk, all while I was wondering how they would respond after they heard the announcement. There would be no more friendly smiles, warm hugs, and casual conversations.

The meeting started, and the opening song came on. One of the elders came up to me and asked for the appeal letter. "I'm not appealing," I said.

"Oh, you're not?"

"No, I'm not." He looked surprised, walked away from me, and right over to another elder. They began to whisper back and forth.

Soon thereafter, another elder approached me and said he was told I was not appealing. My response was: "No, I'm not appealing. Go ahead and make the announcement. Tell your lie." I'm not sure if he heard the last part of my statement but that is how I felt. It felt like a lie was going to be told that night; one that resulted in defamation of character.

I don't recall seeing many people present at the meeting the night their name was announced. But I did go. I don't know if my showing up threw the brothers off, but they were indeed surprised I was there. I would like to believe it was so everyone would not make sense of my presence or at least they could see they could not crumble me. Outwardly, anyway.

What goes on behind closed doors is not the loving, encouraging scenario they paint in the magazines. It is quite the contrast and it was a wakeup call for me. What I read in the past was different from what I experienced that night. There was definitely a double standard.

Even though I realized I didn't stand a chance with the elders in my congregation, I still held out hope that if I involved someone else, someone higher up, the decision would be rescinded and reversed.

Yeah, I grow quite determined when I feel I have been misunderstood or treated unjustly and I was going to make sure I got heard. It was just a matter of timing.

In my entire JW life, I had heard of only one situation in my area where a disfellowshipping was rescinded, and I would be the second.

Nearly two hours later, at the end of the meeting, they invited *so and so* to come up to the stage for an announcement. An announcement made at the end of the meeting is not usually a good thing. I remembered how I'd braced myself for those moments in times past, because nine times out of ten, somebody's name was getting read out. This time it was my name and I sat there, poker face still intact, but very nervous.

The announcement was short and to the point. "Gail Theresa White is no longer one of Jehovah's Witnesses."

The congregation stood, sang the last song, and a final prayer was said. Unlike when I entered just two hours prior, I walked out with not a single person speaking or looking at me. I managed to hold it together.

With those ten simple words, everyone had gotten their cue. They knew what they should do. The shunning and isolation process had begun. This was my new reality.

The appeal was withdrawn, and the verdict stands.

3 | SOLITARY CONFINEMENT

You intended to harm me, but God intended it for good to accomplish what is now being done, the saving of many lives.

Genesis 50:20

Surprisingly enough, I was alright. For the moment, at least. My daughter had moved out the year before and I was an empty nester. As soon as I got in my car, I called her to let her know about how the night had gone. She expressed that she didn't want me to be alone. Another example of how my daughter is such a special and endearing person in my life—and in the lives of many.

So, we met up at the restaurant Chili's for a late-night snack. Spending time with her allowed me to take my mind off what had just happened. It was exactly the distraction I needed. I even felt a bit better and stronger from her presence.

However, I couldn't live at Chili's with my daughter for the rest of my life. I had to go home eventually; the time had come for Sophie and me to go our separate ways…

I walked into my house and said out loud, *Oh Snap!* Realizing things just got real.

Not sure what to do, I sat down to watch TV and casually thought, *well, I guess it's just you and me now, God.* The message I felt back was nice, though: *I'm all you need.* Hmm! Did I just hear that correctly or was I imagining things? I dismissed it and tried to wind down for the night as usual.

Every bit of "I've got this" I'd mustered up was quickly evaporating. The reality that life had just changed, that I couldn't simply pick up the phone and call my friend who I would talk to after the meeting, struck me hard. Rules and restrictions were now in place. My temporary stability started to waver.

Praying to God had given me comfort before, although not always the desired outcome. Furthermore, despite believing I could accept any outcome prior; the stark reality of my new life quickly overwhelmed me. I could not have anticipated its onset being so rapid.

My punishment had just begun, and I was thrown into the pit.

Wow! There was no one to call. My world had shrunk even more than before.

JWs are discouraged and mostly adhere to not forming any genuine friendship with anyone outside the organization. Yes, I knew this in theory. However, how my heart processed it was considerably different. I had never felt so isolated in my life.

Doubts began to surface. This is what the organization desires of someone who is disfellowshipped? What I had just experienced was a loving act? You, alone with your thoughts, must contemplate how you got here and wait for Jehovah's anger and displeasure of you to subside? The thoughts were bombarding me, and I had zero strategies on how to handle it. I had not evaluated my actions as thoroughly as I should have.

Was this all worth it? Maybe not.

The brutal part of my internal dialogue was beating myself up for it all. The logical part wondered, what did you think was going to happen? The harsh voice wondered if God's love was supposed to feel the way I felt it. I was so conflicted.

Finally, the sanest idea I could have had presented itself. *Okay, take your medicine and get some sleep.* I'd been taking Xanax and Ambien for years to help alleviate stress and anxiety.

After tossing the pills down and swallowing them with a glass of water, I waited. I just wanted to go to sleep and forget the whole night. But that didn't happen.

Where was my blissful sleep?

Unfortunately, not even a yawn escaped my lips. It usually worked within 30 minutes, but it was not meant to work that night.

My mind quickly spiraled out of control. How did I get to this point? I brought this on myself. What could my actions have done to make my life better? I felt nothing and my attempts to justify that they misread my heart failed. It was plain as day: I had created a situation there was no going back from.

Early morning crept in—maybe 3 AM—and still no sleep. The reality of isolation was more than my heart and mind could process.

I recalled once researching how many sleeping pills would need to be taken if a permanent end to the pain was necessary; to go to sleep and never wake up. That time had arrived; there were no hopes of the pain and sadness lessening.

If only my eminent end had been better organized. Two things were quickly realized. First, I didn't have enough pills to get the job done. Second, maybe I could take as many pills as I could first, then go sit in my car in the garage and complete the task.

There I sat at the edge of my bed, sobbing. Thinking what were believed to be my last thoughts. Then I heard the words: *Hold on, Gail. I got you. This is not how it ends. You're going to want to see how it ends.*

It was not audible, but it was pleading with me. I knew I hadn't lost my mind, although it felt like it.

I brushed it off and was irritated: *Great, not only do I not have Jehovah's Holy Spirit, now I'm hearing the demons.*

With disfellowshipping, witnesses are told God's Holy Spirit withdraws from them. I'd been taught that all my life. Hearing what I heard was not adding up. It seemed unnecessarily cruel at that fragile moment.

And, as every JW who is well-versed in the publications knows, you've been handed over to Satan once disfellowshipping occurs and a sense of urgency to return to Jehovah is now the motivating factor.

> Watchtower article, "Organized in Harmony with God's Own Book," November 2016, paragraph 14.

> Paul directed the elders to hand the immoral man over to Satan—in other words, to disfellowship him. To preserve the congregation's purity, the elders needed to clear out the "leaven." (1 Cor. 5:1, 5-7, 12) When we support the elders' decision to disfellowship an unrepentant wrongdoer, we help to maintain the cleanness of the congregation and perhaps move the person to repent and seek Jehovah's forgiveness.

Despite my desperation to end it all, God's bigger plan took hold and carried me. Even with my self-condemnation I didn't have the strength to do another thing. I decided to make one last call.

This turned out to be one of the most important phone calls of my life; it was to the crisis hotline.

They answered the phone and asked what was wrong. It was hard to even think of how to answer the question. What could I say? Would they understand what it meant to be disfellowshipped as a JW? Probably not. I simply told the man on the other end I wanted to end it all. However, their training with emotionally vulnerable people was evident. Their goal was to keep me on the phone, as evidenced by the guy talking calmly to me.

He wanted to get me to the ER and asked if he could call an ambulance for me, to which I said "no." My daughter's best friend lived next door. I didn't want to alarm the neighbors and cause a scene, bringing any unnecessary attention that early in the morning.

He urged me to go to the hospital. I wouldn't commit to following his request, but he didn't give up.

This exchange went back and forth.

Finally, I agreed to drive myself there and he called the hospital and told them to expect me.

Sure enough, they were expecting me and got me to a room right away.

Arriving at the hospital brought on a new wave of emotions, yet a sense of relief. It was four in the morning; I could feel the exhaustion and the medicine finally kicking in. I think I felt safe because I wasn't alone at my home.

The counselor questioned me to find out what was wrong and to determine if I needed to be admitted or not. I didn't have the words to tell them what was wrong. How do you explain you were just cast out, cut off from friends and family? This wouldn't make sense to the rest of the world. Still, they kept coming at me, patiently but firmly. They wanted answers…

"Do you have any family I can call?"

"Do you have a pastor I can call?"

"Is there anyone I can call?"

The tears flooded me again. All I could do was shake my head, yes or no, and shrug my shoulders.

These questions were a harsh reminder that I had no one to reach out to. I was disfellowshipped! My entire life had been based on building friendships with JWs only. Now, I wasn't accepted there because I'd sinned badly enough to be cast out.

By the time 10 AM came around, I managed to get some sleep and was told that they didn't see a reason to keep me there.

I was discharged because they didn't feel I was a risk to myself. Not sure if I felt the same way. They never got any answers out of me.

Before long, I was signing a piece of paper promising I would not hurt myself.

I had made it through one of the *DARKEST* nights of my life.

My mom was still weighing on my mind. I didn't get a response to my message the night before. So, I sent her one more text message.

> Hi Mommy, I'm sorry if I hurt you by not telling you directly. That was not my intention. I couldn't talk about it.

She responded with a pulsating heart GIF emoji. It made me smile because she loved emojis and kept up with the latest trends. She even created her own bitmoji. Hilarious!

Then she wrote:

> That's okay. But I am glad you are making use of Jehovah's love this side of the great tribulation because

once it starts the door will be closed, as in Noah's day. I know you will be back soon. See you then.

That was our last conversation, two years ago.

The great tribulation is a time of distress; the precursor to Armageddon.

At this moment, I still believed the same thing. This was all worth it to bring my daughter back to Jehovah, as well. She had not been baptized so she couldn't be disfellowshipped like I was. By showing Sophie the way, hopefully, she would eventually follow my lead.

The disfellowshipping announcement had been on a Wednesday night and it was followed by some agonizing days of self-reflection.

On Thursday I was supposed to go to a meeting with my dad. He called to see if I was on my way, not knowing the announcement had been made. I explained my night in the hospital. He didn't know what to say, other than I knew what I needed to do and to hurry back.

Soon enough, it was Saturday—the day for the next meeting at the kingdom hall, the special annual meeting. I decided to go and had determined in my mind not to miss any meetings, desiring to show humility and repentance. This is how I took steps toward the process of "works befitting repentance."

One part of me was glad to be getting a clear conscience before God, while another part of me was determined to prove how wrong they had been in their decision.

Despite God's presence and guidance during my night of struggle, I was not in a position where I yet appreciated this for the powerful gift it was.

If only...they had decided to publicly reprove me. Everything would have been different. People would have been able to talk with me, although they would have known I had confessed to some wrongdoing.

As I sat through the meeting, I put my phone in silent mode and put it in my purse instead of on my lap, where I normally placed it. It was Saturday, not a time I would usually talk with Sophie.

Four hours later, I left the meeting and once outside, I reached for my phone. I saw at least ten missed calls from her. And there were voice mails. Her voice was sheer panic.

She had left work and was on her way to my house when I called her back. "Sophie, oh my God..."

She was hysterical and screaming, the type of scream that almost sounds like laughter. "Mom, where are you? I've been calling you for hours." "Mom!" She shouted, her voice shaking.

"I'm sorry, there was a meeting today and I turned the ringer off."

"What? I thought you..." Her words trailed off and I knew what she'd thought I'd done. I can't even write the words to finish the sentence all this time later.

Sophie came over to see me. She was still a little shaken and there was a sense of relief that washed over us as we hugged.

I apologized over and over for her having to worry. This was so hard to see and experience. It gave me a taste of what almost was. What if I had hurt my daughter that way because I couldn't handle everything and gave up?

It was evident. I had to fight my way out of this darkness, no matter how difficult it was.

That day, Sophie stayed over at the house and made me the most beautiful card. She's amazing at calligraphy and she pulled out a blank card and started to create something just for me.

So beautiful; it made me cry tears of happiness that day and it still does to this day. That card does not leave my purse.

In my mind, I was still a JW and so I acted the way I should in order to get reinstated.

I stopped using Facebook because most of my friends were JWs and if someone didn't know I was disfellowshipped, I didn't want them to unknowingly interact with me. Doing this could lead to problems for them and for me.

If I was out at the store and ran into someone who didn't know I was disfellowshipped, I did what was required—let them know I was disfellowshipped.

Still…with all the newfound time on my hands, what was I going to do? I needed something, including finding a new job. With working in the family business for almost twenty years and not having a degree, this was a struggle.

Why not go to school?

Two weeks after the announcement, I began the process of enrolling in community college and a few weeks later I was set to go. This moment hit me strangely. What are you doing? It seemed like I was all over the place. A forty-nine-year-old woman going back to college. What was I thinking? Then I started saying the following words:

Watch me soar
Hear me roar
Watch me shine
This light of mine

I was down but not out
As I figured what life is about
Feeling stuck as if in quicksand
All along it was part of the plan

To repair and refine
This negative state of mind
The healing has been slow
And yes, there was blow after blow

But like a butterfly emerging from a cocoon
You will see the change very soon

I am not a poet, but the rhyming words were coming so fast that I pulled out my phone and wrote it down as quickly as I could. It took less than five minutes and revealed my future would be brighter than my present and that I was going to come out of the pit I had toppled into. To this day, this poem remains on the wall above my computer—a reminder of transformation and growth.

Undertones and Implied Messages

Local needs talks are talks that are given by elders or a circuit overseer. During this kind of talk, information is shared about possible challenges specific to a congregation.

In the past, these talks had been given every now and again. Usually within a few weeks of someone being disfellowshipped. They provided members an idea of why someone had been disciplined. Alcoholism, pornography, fornication, and other problems were often spotlighted during these talks. As you listened, it was easy to figure out exactly why someone had been disfellowshipped.

One of these talks were given a few weeks after my disfellowshipping by the circuit overseer. I had become diligent in going to the meetings and I sat there taking it all in. Wow, I couldn't believe my ears. You don't have to read between the lines to receive the message. My confidentiality had been breached. The circuit overseer was not on my committee. The information had not remained in that room.

Feeling betrayed and humiliated, I left the meeting in tears… So much detail from someone who wasn't in the room. I would leave those meetings thinking: *God, you must really be angry with me.*

Having gotten a bit smarter, I had started recording the meetings. Admittedly, I can't say it is me they were referring to specifically and if I suggested it, they would have denied it. They are clever enough not to use a name but devious enough to make sure everyone has a pretty good idea of who they are referring to.

Although therapy was frowned upon, I kept seeing my counselor during my solitary confinement. I never brought religion into our sessions. I just needed an outlet and a pathway to manage all the stress and anxieties the years had placed upon me. My therapist, Susan, did not know I was a JW, much less that I was disfellowshipped. It had never come up in our sessions.

But after this betrayal, I could no longer hold it in. A couple of days after this meeting, I went to my regular weekly therapy session. I let Susan in on my shameful secret and tried to explain what disfellowshipping was and how to JWs, isolation from family and friends were a form of discipline and love. This release led to me weeping uncontrollably.

The information made her gasp and without hesitation, she broke protocol, dropped her notebook, rushed over to where I was sitting, hugged me and began to pray over me. I noticed she was tearing up too. As she held onto me, all she could say was: "Oh sweetheart, I'm so sorry." It was so genuine and heartfelt, and I felt human again.

A hug. A simple, yet powerful expression of human affection can make a world of difference in the life of someone who is experiencing emotional pain. At that moment of vulnerability, the hug was comforting and gave me a sense of safety.

She expressed something which seemed to be a simple truth from her perspective, as well as many others. That disfellowshipping was not a form of love, it was abuse.

For the first time, I allowed myself to accept it as true. I had been put through an abusive process rare to most, but far too common in the JW community. Even one occurrence is one too many.

A renewed sense of self came over me and I gained the resilience I would need to weather the storm that was still brewing.

In retrospect, had I not been in therapy, the night of the disfellowshipping announcement might have gone quite differently. Therapy is not often suggested by the organization and its members are encouraged to look to the elders for help and that Jehovah's organization provides us with our needs and we should look to him for comfort. If we are unhappy, try doing more for Jehovah. Therapy equipped me to process the stresses of life better than the organization ever had. It was not my inactivity that was depressing me, it was this organization and their God that I couldn't seem to please.

Three years later and I'm still in therapy.

That moment with my therapist was just the beginning. I began to experience human compassion at its finest. During a time when I needed the most support, I was at the mercy of men who made the decision, on behalf of God, that I needed to be cut-off from my friends and family.

Over the next few weeks, things started to happen that I could not reconcile or even wrap my head around.

Three events stand out clearly to me in these weeks; each of them serves as a beautiful reminder of how God shows up and provides what we need when we need it most.

This doesn't just apply to me—this is everyone. I have learned God is not partial. If He did it for me, He will do it for you too.

One day, out of the blue, I got a call from an elderly lady asking for Betty. I told her I was sorry; she had the wrong number. She said "oh, okay" and then added: "Before I let you go, I just want you to know that Jesus loves you." The words sent chills through my body and I started to get emotional. Afterward, I was composed enough to thank her for her kind words. Still, not completely in a space where I could accept it, my thoughts were: *How could that be when I don't have the Holy Spirit any longer? Is the devil playing tricks with my mind?*

Not long after that, I decided to treat myself to a facial because Groupon had a great 50% off sale. (This experience is not sponsored – LOL!) I went to get my facial and as the lady was massaging my face, she said: "I hope you don't take this the wrong way, but the Holy Spirit is directing me to give you free facials every month for as long as you need."

I was moved. I'm hearing these people talk about Jesus and the Holy Spirit and it is so different than anything I had ever learned. This truth…made sense on its own. I tearfully and graciously accepted her offer.

Then, I went to get a sandwich for lunch one day and for no reason, out of nowhere, the lady behind the counter says this one is on her.

To some, these events may seem inconsequential. But being on the receiving end of such random acts of kindness, I had begun to see a different side of humanity.

My strength came from complete strangers, who were so-called "worldly people," meaning people who were not servants of Jehovah. Association with "worldly people" could be detrimental to one's spirituality and prospects of everlasting life.

All these things happened to me for no reason I could explain, and at just the point in my life when everything should have been falling apart, it seemed everything was falling into place.

Solitary confinement opened my eyes.

PART II | CONTROL & DETERRENCE

WARNING!

I would like to warn you in advance that if you are not a Jehovah's Witness, the next two chapters may make you feel like you've developed a case of spiritual food poisoning. However, it is necessary for all to know how a witness is trained to think, act, and respond to all aspects of life. So, hang in there with me.

-G

4 | RULES OF THE SYSTEM

*Woe to you, teachers of the law and Pharisees, you
hypocrites! You travel over land and sea to win a single
convert, and when you have succeeded, you make them
twice as much a child of hell as you are.*

Matthew 23:15

To understand this organization, you must understand the
groundwork. The fundamental teaching in the JW system is
that God has a heavenly organization and a visible earthly
organization that was established in 1914. Jesus kicked
Satan and his demons out of heaven, and they were hurled
down to the earth (Revelations 12:9).

"The Bible teaches that God's Messianic Kingdom, a
heavenly government, was established in 1914." The
Watchtower (Public Edition), 2017, No. 5, p. 6.

Therefore, the condition of the world has gotten
progressively worse since 1914. Just after, Jesus inspected
all the groups on earth and chose the Watchtower Bible and
Tract Society as the organization to be the faithful and
discreet slave spoken of in Matthew 24:44-45.

"When did Jesus appoint the faithful slave over his
domestics? To answer that, let us talk more about what
happened at the beginning of the time of the harvest in
1914. As we learned earlier, at that time many groups
claimed to be Christian. From which group
would Jesus choose and appoint the faithful slave? That
question was answered after he and his Father came
and inspected the temple from 1914 to the early part of

51

1919.* (See endnote.) (Malachi 3:1) They were pleased with a small group of loyal Bible Students who showed that they truly loved Jehovah and his Word." The Watchtower, July 15, 2013, paragraph 12, titled "Who Really Is the Faithful and Discreet Slave?"

According to Watchtower, this faithful and discreet slave is known as the governing body of Jehovah's Witnesses. Today, there are eight members of the governing body. The faithful and discreet slave is responsible for giving food at the proper time and are of the anointed class—the 144,000 who will go to heaven and rule from heaven with Jesus.

"Who, then, is the faithful and discreet slave? That slave is made up of a **small group of anointed brothers who directly prepare and give out spiritual food during Christ's presence.**" The Watchtower, (Simplified Edition) July 15, 2013, paragraph 10, titled "Who Really Is the Faithful and Discreet Slave?"

All this literature and the teachings from Watchtower create a goal of every Jehovah's Witness to make Jehovah's heart glad. Admonitions encouraging a healthy fear of Jehovah are never-ending. This healthy fear, which governs every decision, every thought, and every emotion lead to having a clean conscience before Him.

Being a JW means you are part of a worldwide brotherhood and you live a life which revolves around the organization. It becomes your identity and way of life. We knew life as a JW would be difficult. But the reward, eternal life on a paradise earth, would make all the struggles worthwhile.

According to Watchtower, an identifying mark that Jehovah's Witnesses are the true religion is the love they have among themselves.

Emphasis was always to avoid bringing reproach on Jehovah's name by being on guard of how one should act, speak, think, or even dress.

You may be on the outside looking in, or perhaps trying to better understand the dynamics of the JW life for someone you care about and are isolated from. Here's some information about the expectations of a JW in various life matters.

Attending Meetings vs. Managing Life

Regular meeting attendance is vital to one's spirituality. Our attendance showed the extent of our love for Jehovah and the appreciation for the spiritual food he provides through the faithful and discreet slave. Missing one meeting could lead to a habit of missing meetings that would eventually lead to one becoming inactive and "falling out of the truth."

In my situation, my weighty and hectic work responsibilities were exhausting. I was a single mom trying to get by in this temporary system, give my daughter a good life, and be a solid witness. This meant I was on the go from dawn to dusk every day, trying to live a balanced life. It was a juggling act.

In the early days, dropping Sophia off at daycare was a guaranteed dragged-out process. She would cry and didn't want me to leave her there. This tugged at my heartstrings and made it so hard for me to just hand her to the caretaker and leave. Anguishing! I would try to comfort her and tell her: "It's okay, sweetie. Mommy needs to go to work. I'll be back, I promise." She responded with crying and screaming.

Finally, I would leave, also crying and trying to recompose myself as I head to work. Her tortured face was still in my mind. As soon as I arrived at work, I called the daycare to make sure she was okay. They assured me she was fine, and then I could get on with my workday.

Meeting days were the worst—the biggest struggle—always. While there was no official attendance taken, people noticed when you were not there. Whether it was an isolated instance or a pattern of missing meetings.

After work, I would rush to pick Sophia up, eat a little something, maybe cereal, and out the door we went.

After doing the best I could, I sometimes arrived late at the meetings, thankful for enough steam left to make it at all. I was often exhausted, but I made the effort to go anyway, late or not.

From time to time, elders would schedule a "shepherding call" to encourage a witness who may seem to be struggling. Yes, that was me a time or two. Then if it was a big enough concern, a local needs talk came next, addressing issues such as being late, missing meetings, etc. These talks tended to leave me feeling guilty and deflated at the same time. They had no idea what it took for me to get there. The effort didn't seem to matter.

One time an elder felt compelled to comment that maybe I had an issue with time management. I found my voice to give it to him straight. I said: "You have someone at home that cleans your house, does your grocery shopping, cooks your dinner, does your laundry, right? Guess what? When I leave work, I get to go home and do all that and more. And there's only one of me. I'm wearing all these hats that you and your wife share. I do everything." He looked at me with a curious expression, like he'd never considered that perspective before.

The society eventually dropped meetings from three-a-week down to two, realizing that the demands of life were increasing, which made things a little bit easier.

One thing about meetings were women could participate by giving comments or giving talks during the Theocratic Ministry School. Two sisters would be given a topic to research and then would prepare a five-minute presentation. These talks were designed to help witnesses gain confidence in having a meaningful discussion with others about Jehovah and our beliefs. It also taught us how to overcome objections in the door-to-door ministry. For instance, if someone says, "I'm not interested" or "I believe in Jesus," we knew how to overcome this through the training we received.

Field Service

Attending meetings was important because it prepared us for field service. The one thing JWs are known for is going door-to-door. Most everybody has experienced at least once what it is like to answer the door to those two JWs standing there, asking for a minute of your time.

Going out in field service and the amount of time you choose to spend in the ministry depends on what your heart has motivated you to do.

When I first moved to Texas from New York I had more credits than what most kids would have at that age. It led to me graduating high school six months early. Immediately after this, I went into auxiliary pioneering. I did this for about ten months. At that time the requirement was sixty hours a month. I also worked at Walmart part-time, but I needed to make more money and required a few more skills for a better opportunity. So, I opted to enroll in a six-month business school instead of college, since college was frowned upon as being a waste of time. After completing business school, I became a full-time secretary, dropped my pioneering, and went back to being a "publisher," which is someone who averages ten hours a month, enough to remain active.

For much of my life, I had been in training for field service. Field service does become easy for a JW to do, even if they are very shy like I was.

> "We need to help people understand how important it is for them to take their stand for Jehovah and his Kingdom. This means trying to motivate people to make the truth their own by applying what they learn, dedicating their life to Jehovah, and getting baptized. Only then will they survive Jehovah's day." The Watchtower (Study Edition), "Keep Busy During the Last of "the Last Days", October 2019, p.14.

For some, it seems strange to be diligent in door knocking, but it is important to a witness, as it reinforces our love for Jehovah and others. The reminders are endlessly repetitious. Much emphasis is placed on the responsibility of sharing in the preaching work. All the theocratic activities we do is for our salvation and to help in the salvation of others. As implied in Ezekiel 3:17-20, if we warn people and they do not listen, we will not have blood on our hands. I can now identify these activities as "works."

Strangely, although it is taught to do this for different reasons, it does help bring out good qualities in an individual. I'm positive no one in the organization thought they were training me to find my voice to speak out and raise awareness about them. Much less lead me to the truth about Jesus and the Bible.

Baptism

A JW gets baptized to symbolize their personal relationship and dedication to Jehovah.

> "When presenting themselves for baptism, such new disciples confirm that they have disowned themselves and are determined to serve God with all their strength, means, and abilities. (Rom. 12:1) For these reasons, baptism candidates are asked to confirm that they have dedicated themselves to Jehovah to do his will." The Watchtower (Study Edition), "Baptism—A Requirement for Christians", March 2018, pp. 3-7.

I remember making my dedication at sixteen years old, while I still lived in Brooklyn, New York.

My mother had started taking me to the salon to get my hair done. The salon was owned by two biological sisters, who stood out in the crowd because of their beauty.

On previous visits, I had heard these ladies talk about their boyfriends, about going disco dancing, and about all the things they did in their carefree life.

One time, after my mother left to go make dinner, they came up to me and started talking to me about my religion while I was sitting under the hairdryer. I'm not sure what I had said previously to spark this discussion. But I'm pretty sure I had expressed my doubts and they decided this was the perfect opportunity to share their views with me.

They began to tell me I could make my own decisions as to whether I want to be in the religion or not. They were so emphatic, and their dislike for JWs was unmistakable. I felt guilty for whatever comments I made to them. Their approach scared and offended me, and I realized I did not want to become like them. I wanted to be in God's organization.

A few months later, I met all the requirements and was baptized as one of Jehovah's Witnesses, because I truly loved God and wanted to do what was right.

That one interaction drove me deeper into the arms of Watchtower.

Societal Interactions

The association a JW chooses is a matter of life and death. Choosing good associates who are separate from the world was and remains a good choice.

When it comes to dress and grooming, although JWs dress modestly, they don't dress differently. There is no distinction like there are for certain other religions. Since there is a risk of blending in it reinforces an individual's responsibility to keep doing what reflects well on the organization, dressing modestly in the eyes of others and Jehovah.

The same could be true for many things most of society would consider normal; the internet, movies, music, parties.

There are many more examples. Take note that one thing avoiding all these things will do is keep you distanced from any individuals or information which may tell you a different truth than the organization wants you to hear.

One group that pays the biggest price for this is the children. Parents must constantly be on guard about how their child behaves, including at school. How do you tell a child to not build true friendships at school with any child that is not a JW?

Single People

Navigating singleness as a JW can be tricky. For some, being single is a comfortable spot to be in. When you are a single JW and desire to get married, there are some things which work against you more than they would in other religions and parts of society.

I personally discovered the challenges through my years of being single.

Years after I had gotten divorced, a relative tried to set me up with a potential suitor (a JW, of course). He gave this person my phone number and they eventually called. The first thing he wanted to know was how I looked. He asked to see a picture and I directed him to my Facebook profile. I also began talking about my daughter.

"Oh, you have a daughter. So, you were married before?"

"Yes, but I'm divorced." I replied.

He said he had to go and just like that the conversation was over. The end. This call lasted a minute at most.

It was a reminder of how this man was looking for a certain type of person. I did not fit the criteria, and this wasn't an isolated incident. There is a small dating pool in the organization and men are likely to pursue someone without children. This is fine if this is their preference, of course, but it is exhausting if you're someone trying to do the best you can, despite your past. During my entire adult life, from twenty-five on, being overlooked felt like a sucker punch to the gut.

When I followed up with my relative and told him how the call went, he acted surprised and then echoed something I'd heard on and off my entire life: Are you hiding something? Do you need to go to the elders?

People had been accusing me of wrongdoing for a long time. It has made me wonder if trying so hard was even worth it, which in turn made me feel guiltier yet.

JWs are encouraged to widen out in their association and include all. When it comes to socializing with members of the opposite sex who may be single, this is not done casually.

Dating within the organization is serious. For singles who decided to pursue dating, its sole purpose is for marriage being the end goal. You can go out in groups, have a chaperone, or have gatherings at your house. JWs marry "only in the Lord," which means marrying another JW.

Witnesses are encouraged to marry someone who is strong in the faith. Those who are not strong in faith are considered spiritually weak. Signs of a spiritually weak person include not attending meetings regularly, not participating in field service enough or not commenting at meetings. This perpetuates a culture of judging and are the things by which you are judged. This level of scrutiny leads to incredible self-scrutiny more so than evaluating the environment causing it.

Some often settle because they want to be married. For a woman, this can be extra challenging. Fortunately, settling just to say I have a husband has never been an option for me.

A relationship might be nice, but it needs to be the right fit. From this perspective, my life has revealed strength in me to avoid settling just to have an unfulfilling marriage out of desperation.

Marriage

The Bible is the authority on marriage for any Christian. It is expected you will not have sex before marriage. Anyone who goes to a Bible-based church may find similar beliefs and not delve much further into thought about it. For JWs, they often do not realize this is the case. The belief is that others do not think and act quite like they do, even in the capacity of marriage.

Husbands are encouraged to help wives, listen to their ideas, and be thoughtful. It all sounds good on paper. However, when situations arise where one spouse may fall out of favor in the organization or decides they no longer want to be a JW, it can lead to a massive disruption in the family due to the way discipline is managed for wrongdoing and thinking differently.

What most JWs enjoy about marriage is the opportunity it presents to enjoy the celebration. Some have a wedding at the kingdom hall or choose to have it somewhere else, followed by a reception. It can be a big deal if you want it to be! And with not being able to celebrate birthdays and many holidays, weddings or anniversary parties were generally exciting.

Parenting Responsibilities

Being a parent is a serious responsibility and can be stressful. I found being a single JW parent incredibly stressful. Still, my greatest desire was to give Sophia an enjoyable childhood. To do this, I trained her from infancy.

From the moment I went into labor, my hope was to do the right thing by my child that was about to be brought into this world.

JW's are encouraged to train their children from an early age. The *My Book of Bible Stories* was a book of bible-based stories I read to my daughter even while I was pregnant. I would also play the Kingdom Melodies, music produced by the society. I also enjoyed listening to other music, like jazz and R & B.

The pressure I felt to do the right things with my daughter was immense. She was going to be the 5th generation of JWs in my family; this was an impressive lineage and spiritual heritage I was leaving her. It deserved my very best efforts.

Being single and a JW means you also consider a slew of other factors in addition to the standard responsibilities of a parent. Nothing would be more horrible than having your child grow up distanced from Jehovah or worse yet—not wanting to get baptized into the organization.

To prepare a child to go to school, the Watchtower created a brochure for parents to give to teachers before the start of the school year to explain our beliefs. It was titled *School and Jehovah's Witnesses*.

Before each school year, I would go and meet the new teacher and hand them the brochure. A lone child (usually) not participating in Halloween or a Christmas party would stand out to other kids. Honestly, I cannot recall if Sophia just sat to the side during these times or stayed at home. I trusted that she was doing the right thing.

Even though you are juggling a lot as a single parent you are still expected to do your utmost for Jehovah, including meeting attendance, field service, studies, and so on.

In hopes of creating fun experiences and memories for my daughter, I liked having other JW kids over to play in our backyard. They would play games and run around. These get-togethers were fun to watch, and it was good to see all these kids just being kids. Other parents did the same thing.

As my daughter grew older, we found ways to have beautiful adventures together as much as possible. One of my favorites was to hop in the car after field service and head to the zoo or Galveston to chase the sunset. These are cherished and beautiful memories, ones that cannot be tarnished. During these outings, I also taught her how to use a camera to capture the moment.

Another favorite thing to do with my daughter was what I called our *Friday Night Groove*. We would rent a movie or decide on a TV show to watch and eat a pizza. We both looked forward to this so much and the night would depend on if we had to get up early for field service the next day or not. To maintain some sort of balance in my life, we would go in field service every other week.

Connecting with these precious memories are helpful, because not every single moment was a struggle. However, the heavy burdens of trying to fulfill the expectations of the organization are never far from one's mind.

With all the beautiful memories, there are regrets too. Not playing with my daughter enough was one of mine. She would often ask me to play Barbies or board games. "Come play with me, Mommy." I was either cleaning, cooking, or just wiped out from my long day.

Today, I could not be prouder of the beautiful and inspiring young woman she has become. She's engaged to be married and has started on a journey that will take her to amazing places. Her heart is filled with love and she cares about so many things deeply and passionately. To have done all this despite what my life and example have been at times truly helps me identify why the road I am on now is one so worth it.

Higher Education

Going past your basic high school diploma is frowned upon. In a world where you need a degree to do just about anything, this can become very challenging. I lived it out personally by finding out how hard it was to get a job after selling the family business.

Some of the fears of higher education include being exposed to thoughts, ideas, and association that veer away from JW teachings. In my life, pursuing a higher education helped me grow into a better person.

After I was disfellowshipped and decided to pursue a degree, I enjoyed the productivity and activity involved with it. It was therapeutic and relieved my stresses and anxieties a great deal.

When I enrolled, an advisor had cautioned me about how tough it would be. My age combined with my aggressive desire to finish in a year would be challenging. I'm not certain that she was discouraging me as much as warning me, but I needed to go back to school so I went anyway.

School kept my mind occupied and I was in a hurry to finish because time was not on my side. In the end, it took me five semesters to get my associates degree. This accomplishment was good for my self-esteem and it felt amazing to know I could do it, especially at my age and what I was up against.

During my last semester, I stopped in to see that same advisor who initially enrolled me. At first, she said she was busy. I told her I wasn't going to take up her time, I just wanted to thank her for helping me get registered for classes. Then I mentioned I was in my last semester. Now she was interested!

It was comical, really. We talked about the commencement ceremony and the topic got around to commencement speakers. I was curious about how to go about the process. I applied, got a call for the audition and I was chosen to be the commencement speaker!

What was so interesting about it was I realized some JWs may be there. I had seen a few on campus—none of who spoke to me. Would any be in the audience? It turned out, yes, some were.

These people had to listen to me give the commencement address. I was supposed to be broken down and lowly, working toward reinstatement. Yet, there I was advancing. Without my isolation and confinement, these beautiful opportunities would not have been present for me.

This accomplishment was a pivotal moment in my healing. I am grateful for the experience and recognize it took hard work to make it so far. I couldn't adequately explain it at the time, but I am aware that I was being guided by God's loving hand and I could see his fingerprints in everything that occurred up until this point.

I wasn't running away from Jehovah; I was growing toward Him.

Having loved ones around to celebrate that moment, meant a lot to me too. My supportive brother, Abraham and my beautiful cousin, Sophia, had both traveled long distances to surprise me. All the while thinking they were watching me on Instagram live, they had been in the audience the entire time. What a beautiful moment that was!

After I completed college, I could easier see how perhaps the fear of a witness getting a higher education had more to do with developing critical thinking skills and experiencing professional achievements. None of which are beneficial to Watchtower.

Living a simple life is encouraged and opens more time for spiritual activities. This leads to the question of how much time is wasted on striving for material things. Focusing on attaining material things means you cannot be giving your best efforts to Jehovah.

Here's the thing: Without higher education encouraged, people are working minimum wage jobs and don't have a lot of extra money. Many do struggle, making just enough to get by and having nothing to give. The society's desperation to isolate people from non-JW's has created a situation where they are asking more and more for money. Something they said they would never do. In this sense, they really shot themselves in the foot.

There is nothing wrong with teaching children to have a charitable spirit. An animated video, produced by Watchtower, shows a little girl going to buy ice cream. Then she thinks about her kingdom hall and pauses…concluding it is more rewarding to give it away than the ice cream would be. The next scene shows the little girl putting her quarter into the donation box at the meeting.

Even asking adults to donate their rewards points and gift cards have become commonplace now. Or to leave their assets to Watchtower in a will, or even have them be the beneficiary of their stocks and retirement portfolio.

What are all the monies being used for?

One thing they talk about frequently is the need for building more kingdom halls, especially in foreign lands.

The other is more scandalous and remains hidden to the rank and file. There is a need for monies to settle legal cases involving alleged child sexual abuse. Kingdom halls are being sold and volunteers have been released from their duty in order to manage the increasing expense.

Financial Privilege

There is nothing wrong with being able to afford a nice vehicle, a nice home, or wear nice clothes. Doing honest hard work for employers is encouraged. One's diligence and honesty at work can be testimony from a witness that could one day spark an interest in the religion and turn into an informal Bible discussion.

So long as... Living a simple life remains the goal.

Witnesses who set a good example in the organization were interviewed at conventions and assemblies. The stories were usually similar; downsizing to a smaller home, a spouse quitting a job so the other could pioneer, some changed their schedule from a full-time to a part-time job to facilitate spending more time in the ministry and less time working.

The usual sentiment in these presentations was how they were happier than they had ever been, and it brought them closer to Jehovah. These talks usually left many feeling needlessly guilty and wondering if they could do more. It also created a craving for that level of happiness.

There is always a sense of urgency; time is running short.

So, witnesses must make good use of their time in this wicked world to warn people about the impending Armageddon.

Then there is the embarrassment these talks can lead to. Never in my life have I been a wealthy person or someone who can financially relax from week to week. What I have been is a thrifty woman who knows how to seek out a good deal so I can have things I enjoy and can afford. One of these things is my car.

I'm a car girl. The faster the better. I got a good deal on a nice used car a few years back. It was unexpected and a deal I wanted to act on.

Imagine sitting in a meeting where they are discussing the very car you drive. Awkward and embarrassing.

With so much expected of a witness, I took to heart all these high expectations and pondered big questions.

How could I measure up?

What did my actions and intentions say about my relationship with God?

Did I not love Him enough?

Was I not spiritual enough?

The rules had set me up for failure.

5 | THE CASE AGAINST DISFELLOWSHIPPING

You have not strengthened the weak or healed the sick or bound up the injured. You have not brought back the strays or searched for the lost. You have ruled them harshly and brutally.

Ezekiel 34:4

Few words are harsher and have more life-altering implications than hearing you are disfellowshipped. The very people whose blood you share and raised you will turn their backs. Not to be cruel, but because they must in order to remain loyal to Jehovah. Friends who may have laughed with you over lunch just a day before will stop talking to you until you are reinstated. Or at least until you do what is required for the elders to feel you can be reinstated.

Jehovah's Witnesses say that the "judicial action" is not only scripturally necessary to keep the congregation clean, but that it is also loving. How so?

Witnesses fully support the disfellowshipping arrangement because:

1) They believe it is the truth; and
2) They believe it is scriptural.

Consider the following quotes.

___

Watchtower (Simplified Edition), "Are You Convinced That You Have the Truth? Why", September 15, 2014, paragraphs 13-14.

WHY THEY ARE CONVINCED THAT THEY HAVE THE TRUTH

13. How do the Witnesses keep their organization clean?

[13] Our brothers and sisters give many different reasons why they are convinced that they have the truth. One brother who has been serving Jehovah for a long time said: "Every effort is made to keep Jehovah's organization morally clean and undefiled, regardless of who has to be counseled or disciplined." How do Jehovah's people keep this high standard? Each one of them does his best to obey what God says in the Bible and to imitate Jesus and his disciples. (Read 1 Corinthians 6:9-11.)

14. What changes have many people made after they were removed from the congregation? What has been the result?

[14] The Bible directs Christians to remove from the congregation those who refuse to obey God. Happily, thousands later have felt very sorry for their actions and have come back. (Read 2 Corinthians 2:6-8.) Because the Witnesses always use the Bible as a guide for their behavior, the congregations are kept clean. This assures them that their organization is the one that God approves. Although many churches allow their members to do whatever they want, the Witnesses live according to Jehovah's standards. This has convinced many people that Jehovah's Witnesses have the truth.

The last two sentences of the above text are so divisive to the body of Christ. They shamelessly talk about churches, while I have found the opposite to be true. Disfellowshipping is

72

counterproductive and has serious ramifications, both emotionally and spiritually.

Watchtower (Study Edition), "Organized in Harmony with God's Own Book", November 2016, p. 14.

> Paul directed the elders to hand the immoral man over to Satan—in other words, to disfellowship him. To preserve the congregation's purity, the elders needed to clear out the "leaven." (1 Cor. 5:1, 5-7, 12) When we support the elders' decision to disfellowship an unrepentant wrongdoer, we help to maintain the cleanness of the congregation and perhaps move the person to repent and seek Jehovah's forgiveness.

Watchtower (Study Edition), "Why Disfellowshipping is a Loving Provision", April 15, 2015, pp. 29-31 had this to say:

> If genuine repentance is not manifest to the elders who serve on a judicial committee, they must disfellowship the person. At first, we may feel that the decision to disfellowship the wrongdoer is drastic or even unkind, especially if we have close ties to that person. Nevertheless, Jehovah's Word gives us sound reasons for believing that such a decision is a loving one.

I am sad to admit I swallowed this spoon-fed, man-made doctrine and ashamed to acknowledge I once shunned people. Not knowing anything else, I considered this normal.

When I think of my former life as a Jehovah's Witness and what I had contributed to putting other people through, I am saddened. I was clueless as to the psychological torture this caused and really believed it was love. To those people, I offer my sincere apologies. By going along with this mistreatment, I was partaking in judging and for that I am truly sorry. I have asked for God's forgiveness.

One of my brothers, Peter, had been disfellowshipped for about ten years already when my time came. He was baptized at age eleven and probably did not know he could one day get disfellowshipped if he got himself in trouble. How does a child or young teenager prepare themselves to deal with the repercussions of reproving and disfellowshipping?

My brother struggled for many years and was suicidal at one time, himself. But I did not know what went on behind closed doors. He never spoke about it and I never asked. We are admonished to trust the elders because they have God's backing. We saw him struggle and equated it to him "leaving Jehovah." It seemed simple, come back to Jehovah and everything will be well again. I am ashamed I had any part in his struggle. He graciously accepted my apology.

Ten years later, I am experiencing the same thing. He knew from personal experience the effects that shunning can have on someone psychologically. He came by the house or called to check on me every day as my repercussions played out. I would always be polite because, in my mind, I was still a witness, which meant I must limit my association with him.

My goal, despite what had already transpired, was to go back to the organization. Not only to reclaim my friends and family but also to be back in good standing with Jehovah.

I am happy to let you know Peter is doing well today. He has a wife and three sons, who I love very much and am thrilled to spend time with my nephews and watch them grow up. He also has his own business that is doing very well.

What my brother reminds me of is imperative to what I share with you: It took him way too long to recover from the effects of shunning. He was only twenty-two years old; too young to be ostracized.

Watchtower published an article that denounced the Catholic Church for their practice of excommunication, citing it was a foreign bible teaching that had no support in the scriptures. The article is found in the January 8, 1947 Awake titled, "Are You Also Excommunicated?" Only five years later, in 1952, the practice of disfellowshipping was initiated.

Today I wonder how many people were truly repentant in that back room but were disfellowshipped anyway.

There's nothing like being personally railroaded to gain perspective of "the other side of the story."

This teaching does not add up. It's as if they are saying, God may have forgiven you, but we're putting you on probation. In the meantime, the warmth of fellowship is withheld until they are certain that you have suffered enough.

One day, an elder, who I respected very much, called me. He went to a different congregation and hadn't heard about the announcement. When I told him, I was disfellowshipped, he said it was too bad, then started to reason with me.

"You discipline your daughter, right?"

"Right," I said.

"And you discipline her because you love her, right?

"Right," I said again.

"Well, that's the same thing. You're being disciplined by Jehovah because he loves you."

I responded quickly. "Yes, I love my daughter and, yes, I disciplined her when she was younger, but I didn't give her the silent treatment."

There was an awkward silence. He was speechless, as if he had never heard it from that standpoint before.

All he could say was "huh, interesting." The conversation ended shortly after.

He has three kids of his own and I can only hope it made him think. I couldn't imagine not speaking to my daughter for an extended period. There is nothing she could do to make me not want to speak to her for six months to a year to discipline her. Most parents would agree that the silent treatment is not a loving approach to disciplining. This is just another one of Watchtower's faulty reasonings that puts a hole in there already sinking ship.

Repentance is a very important factor in connection with reinstatement into the Christian congregation. A disfellowshipped person is not automatically accepted back into the congregation after a certain amount of time has passed. Before he can be reinstated, his heart condition must undergo a great change. He must come to realize the gravity of his sin and the reproach he brought upon Jehovah and the congregation. The sinner must repent, pray earnestly for forgiveness, and conform to God's righteous requirements. When requesting reinstatement, he should be able to give evidence that he has repented and is producing "works that befit repentance."—Acts 26:20. The Watchtower, "Always Accept Jehovah's Discipline." November 15, 2006, Par. 9.

A disfellowshipped JW must meet the criteria of probation before restoration can be given and allowed back into fellowship. A period of time must go by; a willingness to endure ostracism for a set time demonstrates your humility and a repentant disposition.

This sounds contrary to God, who freely forgives.

Jesus' parable of the prodigal son is very different than the way JWs apply the message from this powerful, well-known story. Here's an excerpt to show you this distinction.

Watchtower, "A Father who is ready to forgive." September 1, 1997, pp. 30-31.

The father in Jesus' parable represents our merciful God, Jehovah. Like the lost son, some people for a time leave the security of God's household but later return.

How does Jehovah view such ones? Those who return to Jehovah with sincere repentance can be assured that "he will not for all time keep finding fault, neither will he to time indefinite keep resentful." (Psalm 103:9) In the parable, the father *ran* to welcome back his son. Likewise, Jehovah is not only willing but eager to forgive repentant sinners. He is "ready to forgive," and he does so "in a large way."—Psalm 86:5; Isaiah 55:7; Zechariah 1:3.

In Jesus' parable, the father's genuine love made it easier for the son to summon the courage to return. But consider: What would have happened if the father had disowned the boy or in an angry outburst told him never to come back? Such an attitude likely would permanently have estranged the lad.-Compare 2 Corinthians 2:6, 7.

Isn't this what Jehovah's Witnesses do when they disfellowship someone? For this reason, many have taken their lives and the retention rate is so low, with only 1 in 3 returning to the organization. The same article continues:

In a sense, then, the father laid the groundwork for his son's return at the time he departed. At times, Christian elders today must remove unrepentant sinners from the congregation. (1 Corinthians 5:11, 13) In doing so, they can begin paving the way for the sinner's return by lovingly pointing out the steps that he can take for future reinstatement. The memory of such heartfelt entreaty has later moved many spiritually lost ones to repentance and has prompted them to return to God's household.— 2 Timothy 4:2.

Here is yet another contradiction and misapplication of scripture. The father didn't send his son away, the son left and returned on his own. And when he returned the scriptures state that when the father saw his son from a long way off, he ran to him.

There were no questions or probationary period.

I appreciate how I have come to know this is how the Father views me. He forgave my sins and removed them as far off as the east is from the west.

What they say is that you must show works befitting repentance. Which means continuing to come to all the meetings where no one talks to you. The elders tell you they can't wait for the day when they can welcome you back into the congregation. This is spiritual abuse and it is not scriptural.

The same article continues saying this:

> "The father also showed compassion when his son returned. It did not take long for him to sense the boy's sincere repentance. Then, instead of insisting on extracting every detail of his son's transgressions, he went about the business of welcoming him back..."

Here again, when you go before a judicial committee, they ask many detailed questions about what you were involved in. Even asking about your spiritual routine and point out how slacking off led to falling into the sin. It's as if JW's are expected to be perfect.

"...and he expressed great pleasure in doing so. Christians can imitate this example. They should rejoice that a lost one has been found. Luke 15:10".

The article concludes with this paragraph:

The father's conduct leaves no doubt that he had long anticipated the return of his wayward son. Of course, that is only a shadow of the yearning Jehovah has for all who have left his household. He "does not desire *any* to be destroyed but desires *all* to attain to repentance." (2 Peter 3:9) Those who repent of their sins can therefore be assured that they will be blessed with "seasons of refreshing ... from the person of Jehovah."—Acts 3:19.

I did not feel this at all. You get this treatment only after you are reinstated into the congregation.

These are man-made directives, not God's Word. Still, JW's insist they are teaching the truth about God's Word.

Furthermore, elders say they do not disfellowship you. They may give you the sentence, but they truly feel it is not them. You disfellowship yourself because you chose to sin. How twisted!

Watchtower, September 15, 1981, par. 25 says: The fact is that when a Christian gives himself over to sin and has to be disfellowshipped, he forfeits much: his approved standing with God; membership in the happy congregation of Christians; sweet fellowship with the brothers, including much of the association he had with Christian relatives.

What you don't see discussed among these articles are the consequences of these judicial actions.

The September 15, 2009, Watchtower, pp.16-20, par. 7 said:

> "It is tragic that some are unrepentant and must be disfellowshipped."

No! What's tragic is how none of the articles address the undue mental anguish, distress, humiliation, emotional trauma, feelings of rejection, chronic PTSD, depression, and ultimately suicides that occur as a result of this cruel act of social alienation they call "discipline."

How could an organization that claims to be so loving be oblivious to the psychological damage they inflict? Sadly, many witnesses never connect the two. If ever a connection is made, it is met with indifference.

I do not know the suicide rate among JW's, but I have met many who lost a loved one to death by suicide due to shunning. This information is kept so confidential. Maybe they know at Watchtower or perhaps they are afraid to know.

In most suicide cases, you never find out any reason at all unless a family member shares it. They seldom do.

Disfellowshipping is not a loving arrangement. It has no scriptural basis and has dangerous consequences.

The question then arises: Is disfellowshipping a human rights violation or freedom of religion protected under the First Amendment?

Some disfellowshipped persons have taken the Watchtower to court on the basis that their disfellowshipping caused them financial ruin. Some JW employers choose to let a disfellowshipped person go and vice versa; employees quit if the owner is disfellowshipped. Witnesses can choose to stop doing business with JW owned companies and many have suffered financial loss as a result. Watchtower has won several of these cases because of the First Amendment clause. Some of these cases have gone as far as the Supreme Court. The ruling is usually in favor of Watchtower, citing that the court cannot tell them how to run their "business."

There is no justice for those who have suffered because of this organization, but perhaps there is another method. Human rights violation!

The United Nations adopted the Universal Declaration of Human Rights (UDHR) in 1948.

Article 16, subsection (3) states:

> "The family is the natural and fundamental group unit of society and is entitled to protection by society and the State."

However, Watchtower says:

> "*Respect the discipline of Jehovah.* His arrangement can bring the best long-term outcome for all, including the wrongdoer, even though the immediate effect is painful. (Read Hebrews 12:11.) For example, Jehovah instructs

us to "stop keeping company" with unrepentant wrongdoers. (1 Cor. 5:11-13) Despite our pain of heart, we must avoid normal contact with a disfellowshipped family member by telephone, text messages, letters, e-mails, or social media." Watchtower, "The Truth Brings, Not Peace, But a Sword." October 2017, paragraph 19.

Article 18 states:

"Everyone has the right to freedom of thought, conscience and religion; this right includes freedom to change his religion or belief, and freedom, either alone or in community with others and in public or private, to manifest his religion or belief in teaching, practice, worship and observance."

However, Watchtower says:

"No one should be forced to worship in a way that he finds unacceptable or be made to choose between his beliefs and his family." Awake, "Is It Wrong to Change Your Religion?" July 2009, pp. 28-29.

These contradictions startle me. If someone leaves the organization or decides not to return, their family—their own precious flesh and blood—can no longer be a support system to them. This is meant to manipulate someone into coming back to the organization. You either remain estranged from your family or give in and get back in line. This is a violation of human rights. Not to mention common decency.

When "human rights" has been taken from you it alters you in a way which temporarily blinds you. You cannot see what is happening until you reach such a low that it takes an act bigger than your strength to change the tide—an act of God.

The rights violated by the policies of the Watchtower organization are immense and strip a human of much individuality and dignity. The right to:

- Choose your own religion
- Have your family
- Experience a direct relationship with God

So how common is disfellowshipping? The Watchtower (Simplified), "Are You Convinced That You Have the Truth? Why", September 15, 2014, paragraph 13 states:

> Only a relatively small number of Witnesses have refused to follow God's standards of right and wrong and have had to be disfellowshipped, that is, removed from the congregation. The majority of Jehovah's Witnesses live in a way that is clean in Jehovah's eyes. Many who in the past did things that God does not approve of have changed and now follow God's standards.

The above quotation cites the very reason I could no longer play their game. Going along with it tells others I "refused" and had to be "removed." Disfellowshipping is a scare tactic, a bullying strategy and it is psychological abuse. During this period, you are silenced and cannot otherwise defend yourself.

One can either make the choice to go along with it or walk away. I chose to walk away.

It's important to point out how Watchtower spends an excessive amount of time writing about this practice for something that happens to such a small percentage of witnesses. What do you think the reasoning behind this is? The very thing that led to me writing this book is a big clue: One is liable to come to the light and wake up to the truth.

In November 2016, Watchtower released a brochure titled *"Return to Jehovah."* This brochure is basically a plea for those who have strayed, whether inactive or disfellowshipped, to return to the organization and confess their sins to Jehovah. This is step one.

Step two is a direct quote from the brochure, found on pages 10-11:

> "Jehovah has provided congregation elders who have been trained to help repentant sinners restore their friendship with Jehovah. When you approach the elders, they will use the scriptures and offer heartfelt prayers to soothe your heart, lessen, or remove your negative feelings and help you to heal spiritually."

Nowhere in this brochure does it say there may be a possibility you might get disfellowshipped. To me and to many others, this brochure is misleading. It appears in a loving tone, but it points to a rude awakening.

Furthermore, my conscience will not allow me to go along with such misguided innuendos or ignore them. This unscriptural method of control is harmful, heartless, and vile.

I worry for those who remain in the organization out of fear. Do they learn to cope? Some do, but this is not true of all. Others will choose not to contemplate anything which challenges what they have been taught.

Absolute and complete obedience is expected in this authoritarian totalitarian society. Respect and gratitude for the elders are expected without question.

The theme of the 2019 Regional Convention *Love Never Fails* is so hypocritical, in that it teaches attendees that shunning is loving.

Here is an excerpt from a talk, *Display Unfailing Love...To Those Taking the Lead.*

> "The second way we can show love to those taking the lead [the elders] is found in 1 Corinthians 5:11, where it says that we should support the judicial decisions of the elders by having no association with disfellowshipped persons, not eating with them, not even saying a greeting to them. Do we realize that going against this scriptural direction is disrespectful of the elders and is unloving? Why? Well, it undermines the efforts of Jehovah and the elders to help these ones and to protect the congregation. Failing to do so can cause great harm. So, don't let your love for a wrongdoer cause you to act in a misguided and unloving way."

Just stunning that this is the spiritual food I used to feast on. When I heard this, I understood and realized one of the most effective tools the Watchtower hierarchy had. They have a platform to try and manage dissent within the organization. Basically: Do not question the elders! Questioning the elders and the governing body is equivalent to questioning Jehovah.

The indoctrination of these teachings presented as coming from Jehovah, flows constantly. This is what brainwashing looks like. To prevent belaboring this point, I have included a few more references to these viewpoints in Appendix A.

When all this may feel confusing, turn to Jesus for clarity. He is the embodiment of love and a master teacher through illustration and example.

In trying to reason with me, someone once asked me which love was more important? Love for Jehovah or love for me? Huh? What an interesting question. The person must have thought I was asking them to choose between me or Jehovah. They quoted the scripture: "You must love Jehovah your God with your whole heart and with your whole soul and with your whole mind." By quoting this scripture, the person was expressing their loyalty to Jehovah.

I wanted to understand this scripture in the context that it was being used in. I found three references from Matthew 22:37, Mark 12:30, and Luke 10:27.

Out of these three references, Luke's account was the most detailed. One day, an expert of the law tried to test Jesus by asking him: "*What must I do to inherit eternal life?*" At Luke 10:27, Jesus answered: "*'Love the Lord your God with all your heart and with all your soul and with all your strength and with all your mind'; and, 'Love your neighbor as yourself.'*" Jesus was directly quoting Deuteronomy 6:5.

The question now is who is your neighbor? Jesus answered by giving them the parable of the Good Samaritan at Luke 10:30-37. A man was attacked by robbers and left for dead. The scriptures say he was passed by a "priest" and a "Levite." The scriptures also say these two men avoided the man by passing on the other side. But a third man, a Samaritan, stopped and helped the wounded man. To make his point, Jesus asked:

> *"Which of the three do you think was a neighbor to the man who fell into the hands of robbers?" The expert in the law replied, "The one who had mercy on him." Jesus told him, "Go and do likewise."*

Love is more than a feeling; it is the most powerful emotion a human being can experience and express as a human virtue that is based on compassion, affection, and kindness.

Love is such a complex emotion that the Greeks had four different words for it.

Agape, which is divine love.

Storge, which is familial love.

Eros, which is romantic love.

Philia, which is friendly or platonic love.

To get to the bottom of this, I researched each of these Greek words. What intrigued me most is that the love we are commanded to show God and our neighbor are both the same—*Agape love*. They are one and the same. There is no distinction between the love we have for God and the love we have for our neighbor. We are to have divine love for God and our neighbor.

So how can we love God and shun a human being at the same time? And why would God, in all his representation of love, ask us to shun another?

These actions are hardly divine or merciful, much less compassionate.

In the Good Samaritan parable, the way the priest and Levite pass by the victim is like the way Watchtower says disfellowshipped ones should be treated.

Yet Watchtower says to avoid contact.

> "A simple 'Hello' to someone can be the first step that develops into a conversation and maybe even a friendship. Would we want to take that first step with a disfellowshipped person?"   Watchtower, September 15, 1981, page 25.

This teaching is in stark contrast to the command to love your neighbor. Disfellowshipping is unkind and cruel; it is spiritual abuse. The disfellowshipped are discarded, left on the side of the road for dead, with their reputations tarnished and slandered. Being wounded this way is an unacceptable human treatment.

How can anyone reconcile the action of disfellowshipping with that of divine love? Indeed, it is irreconcilable, because they are contradictory. Legalism does not promote love.

In the end, their hearts couldn't tell what was in mine. Was I repentant? How was I going to prove such a thing to them if I hadn't already? And why would I show it to "them," and not God?

So, what would it cost The Watchtower Bible and Tract Society to give up this unloving and unscriptural practice?

One word: Control!

Disfellowshipping taught me many things; none of which the organization wished for me to know.

6 | THE PAROLE HEARING

For I know the plans I have for you," declares the LORD,
"plans to prosper you and not to harm you, plans to give
you hope and a future.

Jeremiah 29:11

Three months had passed since the judicial committee hearing. I decided it was time to send "the letter." It was simple and concise.

> *Please accept this letter as a request for*
> *reinstatement. There have been no changes since*
> *the judicial committee hearing. I look forward to*
> *your response.*
>
> *Sincerely,*
>
> *Gail*

Compared to other lengthy letters I've heard some people write, this was as short and sweet as it gets. I saw no need for a long drawn out letter. I'd laid it all out there and bared my soul at the meeting where I was disfellowshipped. I was neither going to grovel nor beg. I knew in my heart that God had forgiven me well before I approached them. I could not reconcile what purpose this probationary period served.

I handed it to one of the brothers at the meeting. No one acknowledged the letter. It seemed my request was ignored.

As time passed, it became evident they either wanted me to wait longer or to write another letter.

So, I started wondering how people who left "the truth" were doing. I had no point of reference. All we heard from the stage and the publications were the sad stories of those who hit rock bottom. Nothing goes right in their life and eventually they end up crawling back to Jehovah.

Not having any answers was a restraint for me. I certainly could not handle any more disappointments in my life.

As my mind wandered during one of the meetings, a thought occurred to me. *I wonder why they call it "the truth?"* All my life I had referred to this religion as "the truth." Instantaneously, John 14:6 came to mind. I opened my Bible and read it as I sat in the kingdom hall.

> *"Jesus answered, "I am the way and the truth and the life. No one comes to the Father except through me."*

Wow! There it was. It was like I was hearing it for the very first time. It was a eureka moment for me. A lightbulb went off. *"Jesus is the truth. Not this religion, just Jesus!"*

Something shifted in me that night.

I kept going to the meetings faithfully.

Not a single word.

Weeks began to go by.

Four months passed since I turned in the letter. Finally, an elder tapped me on the shoulder and asked if they could meet with me after the meeting. *Oh great!* There was just one major problem. I was wide awake!

At the time, I didn't know there was a term for what was happening to me, all I knew was I had become fully aware that something was off and decided I wanted out, knowing full well what I was giving up and what it was going to cost me.

I had witnessed the lies and experienced the disparity for myself. What is written in the publications and what happened behind the scenes did not harmonize. It wasn't sitting well with me and I was now faced with the biggest decision of my life.

I went into a full-on panic attack.

Thoughts of me meeting with the three again, of being reinstated, of them announcing my reinstatement and everyone acting like all was well again, began to overwhelm me.

When one is reinstated, another announcement is made from the platform, which is everyone's cue that friendships can now be resumed. The thought of those who had shunned me suddenly talking to me again, welcoming me back, hugging me as if nothing had happened, not even skipping a beat, and going through all these platitudes with the usual enthusiasm sickened me.

The reality was, I'd done well without them and I was in a good place mentally. Great things were happening in my life, and I hadn't felt abandoned by God despite what I had been taught. I felt closer and more connected to Him and no one could take credit for that. The outside world started to make sense to me, while the JW world was becoming more of a fantasy, an alternate universe.

I was never a fake JW. I was all in and really believed. I wasn't going to start faking it now. My conscience would not allow me to be a party to their games any longer. I had seen it for what it was.

How did I reach this turning point? It had only arrived three days before the request to meet.

I had taken care of some business for my dad prior to my disfellowshipping. The package had returned, and I sent him a text message to let him know I would leave it at the front door. At the last minute, I decided to take the package back into the house so he would have to ring the doorbell, which he did.

It had been seven months since we last saw each other. I had lost a significant amount of weight and I wanted him to see that I was doing well, you know, just in case he was curious. I wanted to see him as well. I missed my dad.

I opened the door and all he said was: "I hear you're going to all the meetings." I said yes and that I hadn't missed a single meeting. He asked if I had turned in my letter for reinstatement. I told him yes, four months ago and I hadn't heard anything back.

With some excitement, he said: "Turn in another one."

I thought I knew where his encouragement was coming from. You see, the meetings lately had been about showing humility, helping ones who have fallen to get back up, and being careful about causing others to stumble. In addition, the mid-week lessons for the past two weeks were discussing the Pharisees and their rigid laws. During these talks, I noticed the elders were visibly uncomfortable. Hmm!

Without hesitation, I answered: "No. I'm not going to beg."

He threw his hands in the air and said: "I got to go." He turned and walked away…and…as I watched my dad walk down my driveway, it hit me. There was no love.

How could this be love? This arrangement has nothing to do with love and was not of God. This religion had produced people who couldn't feel anything. No empathy, no mercy, and no compassion.

My dad walking away from me that day, frustrated because I wasn't going to turn in another letter, was the last straw.

That. Is. What. Woke. Me. Up.

The scales had fallen from my eyes.

My Last Day in Court

I was armed with my newfound confidence and had arrived at the realization that what I'd latched onto my entire life was not and could not be God's one true organization. However, when I entered the backroom I remained visibly shaken.

This is the same room where we met seven months ago, and the process began. Again.

I knew the questions they would ask…

Have you repudiated your bad behavior?

Do you understand and appreciate why you were disfellowshipped?

How are your study habits?

How do you feel about what you've done?

How do you feel about your relationship with Jehovah?

The first meeting, I completely trusted the brothers and was confident that they only had good intentions towards me. But after everything that occurred, I wised up and decided to record this meeting.

This is how that meeting went.

Elder 1: "We have seen how you are very faithful in coming to the meetings. Certainly, I know that that takes a lot of effort. It shows, of course, how you are looking to Jehovah to regain the spirituality you had. So, we just wanted to hear from you and get your feelings on how you feel like you are doing."

I replied that I was doing good and mentioned I had turned in my reinstatement letter in mid-January, stating nothing had changed since the judicial committee hearing and that is still the case. Meaning, I was not involved in any wrongdoing.

"But if I could, I would like to request that [*name of District Overseer*] be at this meeting." He was a former circuit overseer, now district overseer and someone who I had respected and felt he had been fair in the past. In my mind, I believed a person who had not been in that room before would see the injustice and realize a mistake had been made.

Elder 1: "Okay, ah, we can contact him." He continued: "So again, why is it that you are asking for this person...because we want to know how you feel like you're doing spiritually, how you feel like you've grown spiritually, how you feel like you're being strengthened."

"Strengthened!" "Grown!" In my head, I shouted: "Are you kidding me? I've been isolated from friends and family for over seven months—the only community I'd ever known. This was supposed to strengthen me? That is what this is about? I nearly ended my life over this...you idiots!"

I was livid, but I kept my composure and answered more reasonably: "I feel Jehovah's forgiveness and I feel that he has granted me a clean conscience and I accept his forgiveness. Beyond that, I don't feel safe."

There. I had said it. And they were not getting anything else out of me.

"You don't feel safe, you don't feel safe with us, here?" he asked. (If he had pearls, he would have clutched them.)

Elder 2 stepped in and asked what the District Overseer would do?

I paused and answered: "I hope to feel a little safer."

Yes, I was being evasive, but I had lost all respect for these men and I was done with being bullied and pushed around. Done with living by their man-made guidelines, as if I were a helpless drone. I felt empowered, although still shaking. From this negative state, if I let my guard down, my next reaction would have been a 10. So, my best bet was to keep my cool and play along, making them feel superior.

Then Elder 2 threw me a curveball: "He's no longer the District Overseer; there is no district overseer anymore and he's not in the circuit work either."

That position was eliminated, and he was an elder in another congregation.

Oh great! I had been inactive that long that I didn't know the position of District Overseer no longer existed and the structure had changed.

The hierarchy was Elder, Circuit Overseer, District Overseer, Branch Overseer, etc.

Learning that he wasn't available was a letdown. I started to feel hopeless again, like I was completely at their mercy.

I was optimistic that someone who knew about the situation I had been enduring for the past few years would stand up for me, speak up. But no one came forward.

Elder 2 continued: "The decision regarding the discipline you received is not what we're here to go over again. You submitted your request for reinstatement and our concern now is determining if that's possible. So, I'm concerned about why you would be scared or fearful of us. Is there something we've done that would make you fearful?"

I didn't answer.

Finally, Elder 3 joined the conversation and asked if I was feeling okay because he noticed I seemed tense.

No, I was not okay. I was angry, annoyed, irritated...the process these men had put me through was sold to me all these years as love. Instead, it was an abusive, overreaching display of their authority and power.

I answered and said I was fine.

I could barely finish my sentence when he quickly dismissed it and continued speaking.

Elder 3: "My one concern is…do you?... Here is what I wanted to ask you to comment on if you will, just to express your feelings."

My physical reaction to this current situation was irrelevant to him.

Zero concern! Zilch!

Elder 3: "At the time when we met with you, my question that is lingering is, did you fully appreciate the reason why you were disfellowshipped? Have you come to terms with…or do you feel maybe the action was not justified?"

Elder 2 had just said they were not here to go over what was discussed in the first meeting and reiterated *they* wanted to know how I was doing spiritually.

But Elder 3 couldn't help himself. He had outstanding questions and he wanted answers.

"That's not my decision to make. I accepted the discipline," I said. I reminded them it was a 5+ hour meeting and that it was a lot to process. "I opened up a lot and I left here feeling more hurt than when I first got here."

Elder 3 continued to press me for an answer: "Do you see how the decision was…because we are just here representing

Jehovah. Our role…and really and truly the Bible says that the decisions that are made are already made in heaven when the elder body meets with you because we are influenced by Holy Spirit and the scriptures in arriving at our conclusions." (Insert eye-roll).

No, you're influenced by your managers manual, oops, I mean elders manual, *Shepherd the Flock of God.*

Here is another scripture they twist to fit their policies and use to their advantage. Jesus said at Matthew 16:19 that "whatever you bind on earth will be bound in heaven, and whatever you loose on earth will be loosed in heaven."

Elder 3: "But have you been able to understand…have you come to terms with why the action was necessary?"

Exasperated at his persistence, I said: "Yes, I was prepared for it before I got here. The setting, the manner of delivery was more painful than anything. I'm not questioning the decision."

Nothing I offered, no expression or angst, was enough for them. There was a clear disconnect.

He [Elder 3] continued to press in: "It's not a matter of questioning. But I want to know if, have you come to the point where you understand, recognize and see why Jehovah, if he were here, would have said 'this is why this was necessary.'"

Unbelievable! I could not believe how much this dude was pushing me at that moment. I didn't want to blow my cover.

"Yes, I made up my mind for that decision before I even got here, even though I had already felt like Jehovah had already forgiven me. But I accepted the decision and once you said I was dismissed, and I left. I did not question you brothers or anything. Correct?"

He continues his prodding as if I was the one not getting it.

Sighing and exasperated, Elder 3 is relentless: "Yes. So, the reason and the direction for my questioning is…have you got the mind of Christ…have you got the mind of Jehovah on why it was taken? Do you see why and harmonize your thoughts with, 'yea, you know, I didn't understand before, but I have come to understand that now.'"

"Yes. I understood then and I understand even more clearly now."

He continues pushing his argument: "Okay. So if we're representing Jehovah and we are merely carrying out instructions Jehovah has given us as responsibilities to carry out and you have come to the point where you recognize that, you harmonize your thinking with that, then we should merely be Jehovah's agents that you're looking at Jehovah saying we are here, but it's really Jehovah that made that decision. So if we are now here, the same three men, who were representing Jehovah then and we're representing Jehovah now, and when you're looking at us, you're really, let's say, looking at Jehovah then…we're now meeting with you because we want to know where have you gone from the date when we met with you until now?"

"Yeah, I never missed a meeting…"

Elder 3 interrupted: "Yeah, I know, we commend you for that."

But I kept talking... "I was here for the announcement; I get here early…"

He interrupted again: "Yeah, the question is, why would you now be saying there is some fear of us three men? We're Jehovah, we're representing Jehovah."

Did you catch that? I did and I didn't flinch because I wanted to see if he would correct himself. He didn't and it wasn't a slip of the tongue either. This was the first time I had heard an elder say they were Jehovah.

Elder 3 repeats: "What is it that we have done that may have made you feel uncomfortable?"

And there it is, he's still trying to get me to say why I am requesting a fourth person be in the room. The pious, arrogant, authoritarian style is mind-blowing to me.

I wanted to address the breach of confidentiality, but only with another person in the room. I would not get to address it in this meeting. I'd have to be patient with that topic.

"Again, I don't feel comfortable revealing it here unless there is someone else neutral."

Elder 3: "So, you're not seeing us as men who are simply representing Jehovah here?"

His persistence was infuriating, but I calmly said: "That's not the case. I think you're trying to coax something out of me."

Elder 3 retaliates: "No, I'm just trying to understand why you would say something like that if you really fully understand what we're doing, what this whole process is about and you're harmonizing your thinking that this is Jehovah's way of doing things, why would there be a problem?"

Looking away in frustration, there was a sarcastic chuckle as he said: "I'm not clear. I don't get that."

He had finally conceded

These men are given so much power. They are used to doing the bullying, getting their own way and not being challenged. They did not know how to handle me. The idea of me standing my ground and not giving up the information was perplexing to them.

He was not getting the answer out of me that he wanted to hear—the one that would satisfy his curiosity.

These men were not my shepherds.

My unswerving determination in words made no sense to my fragile weak appearance.

After another five minutes of scriptural counsel on disfellowshipping, Elder 2 says: "We have no joy in disfellowshipping anybody and we probably go home more hurt than anybody, because that's not an easy thing for us to have to do."

How disconnected and emotionally inept these men were. They lacked basic human empathy and compassion. These men are not trained psychologists. Yet they easily make decisions that altered peoples' lives mentally, emotionally, physically, and spiritually.

Elder 1 jumped back in: "We're doing the best we can with us being imperfect men... to follow Jehovah's direction and what he has set in his organization in what to do and what to follow."

So why are you judging? I thought to myself.

Now they wanted me to accept their imperfection. Aren't we all imperfect, yet they are judging me like they have no flaws?

It is unacceptable to me that the allowance for imperfection works one way but not the other.

Their "imperfections" ruin lives. It results in depression, loneliness, suicide, and other things because vulnerable people become isolated.

These men said they'd prayed for Holy Spirit to guide and direct them in the previous meeting. This messaging is also preached from the platform, as well. Now these three were suggesting that perhaps they got it wrong, that Holy Spirit misled them. No, it doesn't work that way.

Elder 1 went on to say: "You did submit your letter in January, and we had met with you at the end of September. So that's just very little time between when we met with you and the decision."

A probationary period? That sounded more like a penal system than shepherds of God appointed to help readjust a person and help them heal spiritually.

"I submitted it because that's what I honestly felt. I actually wanted to turn in my letter the week after the announcement. But I didn't think there was a time limit."

Again, Elder 1: "There is not a time limit. But what is a factor is…the length of time…the degree of deviation."

"That's not to take away anything from your meeting attendance and your feeling that you've been forgiven from Jehovah. We understand that that's strictly personal. That is between you and Jehovah, just like all our relationships are personal between us and Jehovah. The forgiveness may be there. But does that mean that immediately, the next day, that things are going to be reflected like that? The most important thing is your relationship with Jehovah and how you feel. And if you feel like you're in this forgiveness and whatever wrong you have done, you thought about and repudiate it…know that…that forgiveness will ultimately be reflected by Jehovah's representatives."

This group was nothing more than a legalistic, pharisaical organization and I didn't belong.

Everyone in the organization knows there is an unspoken time limit. Anywhere from 6-months to a year, although they will deny it. This is what goes on behind closed doors. This arrangement does not align with God and is hardly a prodigal experience. The father in Jesus' parable ran to his son with open arms and welcomed him back.

Elder 2 stepped back in to say: "Keep in mind too, Gail, Jehovah can read hearts. He knows everything about you, we can't. We have to be careful. Sometimes a pretense can be made on the part of the person, but we can't tell that. We don't know what a person is doing or not doing…"

I interrupted and said: "I'm not a pretentious person. What I revealed in the previous meeting was my heart."

Processing all this was like separating food in a blender. Everything mixed together as I retraced the feelings of torment from the judicial committee meeting. Despite the intensity of it, I recalled it clearly. As I sat in front of these men—again—I couldn't believe the contradictions I heard. On one hand, they say my relationship with Jehovah is personal and on the other they are trying to discern if I am truly repentant.

Again, I asked myself, where is the Holy Spirit in all of this?

Things had never been clearer to me than they were now.

I was back, baby! The warrior, the fighter, the "I'm-not-backing-down" Gail was back. My fragile appearance had made them think they could bully me and get their way.

After about 25 minutes, they finally gave up and Elder One said they would get back with me.

They never did.

Turning Fifty

Six weeks passed by from that meeting and I was about to turn fifty, the big 5-0. What a time that was. I was not technically a JW anymore, although I was still attending the meetings and working very hard to get back in.

A milestone was approaching, and I wanted to commemorate it.

To bring you up to speed about my inventory of human interaction at this point:

- Shunned by friends
- Shunned by family
- I had my amazing daughter Sophia, plus my brother Peter and his family.

Still...I wanted to mark this occasion of turning fifty and so I let my daughter make the arrangements. She chose the Cheesecake Factory. As I wondered who was going to be there, I thought, *this is going to be pathetic.*

When I arrived, the party included my brother, Peter, along with one of his friends; Sophia was there with her now fiancé and her friends. They greeted me with 50 roses and a balloon with just the number 50 on it. (I had asked my daughter to find a balloon that didn't say "Happy Birthday.") There were also cards and gifts. I was touched and it felt good to be celebrated for one day. Yet, I felt guilty at the same time.

As I looked around the table and took in the experience of my 1st birthday, I noticed I was surrounded by "worldly people," people who according to Watchtower are "bad association" and not my real friends, simply because they are not JWs.

This is the same group of friends from Sophia's childhood— the ones I used to caution her about. Every day when I dropped her off at school, I would say: "Sophia, now remember you are one of Jehovah's Witnesses and these people at school are not your real friends. Your real friends are at the kingdom hall."

Yet, here they were celebrating with me. They showed up to support me and showed up for my daughter simply because she asked. It brought tears to my eyes because, for the first time in my life, I was experiencing unconditional love.

Despite my warnings, Sophia developed a strong network of friends, friends since childhood, friends that show up for everything. Their tight bond was special. Together, they were able to support and celebrate each other through the victories and the losses. Every graduation, promotion, birthday, engagement, wedding, baby shower, the same girls were there. This is what true friendship looks like.

These friends gave me a memorable experience that night and it's a beautiful memory; one that I will cherish for a long time.

My aunt also surprised me for my birthday by having flowers delivered to my house. She had never been a JW, but she remembered when my mother became one.

I called to thank her for the flowers and told her I was awake and not going back. She revealed to me that she had been praying for us all these years, ever since my parents got married, that we would wake up and realize we were in a cult. This alerted my senses because it was the first time I had ever heard this word in the context of my religion.

She also shared stories of the past that I had never heard before; what life was like for them as children.

They celebrated Christmas, birthdays, and all the holidays. Christmas was a special occasion, one where the scent of the tree permeated the house. The house was decorated with lights and filled with wonderful feasts and lively music. Although there were already presents under the tree, my grandfather would take all the children to the toy store on Christmas Eve, to pick out one item of their choice. In the words of my aunt, they were spoiled.

Spoiled? Yes, Spoiled!

I knew none of this and I was astounded. My mother? Really? I wondered why she never mentioned any of this to us growing up.

From what my aunt shared with me and coming off the good feeling which came with being celebrated for one day, I wondered what made her give that up to become a JW.

My special day was over, and I went to the meeting the next day, Sunday, still trying to figure out the best way to make my final exit. My heart was no longer there. Maybe I was just trying to reconcile the fact that I had made a conscious decision to walk away from my family and friends for good. To walk away from the mind control and the manipulation; saying goodbye to the past.

I was also leaving behind the teaching of "Where will I go?" Leaving the organization is equivalent to leaving Jehovah. We had been convinced through the teaching that there was nowhere else to go. We had also been taught that the organization is the only one spreading the good news and preaching all over the world. No other religion came close or had anything in place as the Witnesses had. And that:

> "Living without the help of God's organization and his standards would result in unhappiness and misery." Watchtower (Study Edition), "Organized in Harmony with God's Own Book", November 2016, paragraph 6.

Then there was always the disclaimer that although not perfect, this organization is as close to the truth as one can get. So, if you leave "the truth," where will you go? To Babylon the Great, false religion? For this reason alone, many end up staying. This prevailing message has always been reinforced by their use of John 6:67-68, in which the NWT version states:

> "You do not want to leave too, do you?" Jesus asked the Twelve. Simon Peter answered him, "Lord, to whom shall we go? You have the words of eternal life."

There is just one problem. When I looked the Scripture up in the Bible it clearly references "to whom shall we go," not "where."

When read in context, the accurate application of that scripture is, if we leave Jesus (not an organization) what other options do we have?

It was time to rip off the band-aid and be done with this once and for all and I wouldn't be going anywhere else.

The Watchtower study this week was about, you guessed it, disfellowshipping...again. Ugh! Except this time, it is suggested that this disciplinary action is both for teaching and punishment.

I had decided ahead of time I was only staying for the talk and would leave before the study started. I couldn't sit there and listen to that anymore, especially when you are the only person in the audience who is disfellowshipped.

This meeting was different. I was restless, I couldn't sit still, my legs were so jittery, and I kept shifting in my seat. Although the talk was only 30 minutes, it felt like hours and I couldn't wait to get out of there.

As soon as the transition song started, I bolted for the door. I think I tripped over somebody, but I kept going. When I got outside into the warmth of the sun, I took a breath of fresh air and felt relieved to be outside of that building.

In time, I would realize I had not left God, rather I was moving into the light, growing toward Him. I left an organization and I never looked back.

Now I was hearing things differently.

PART III |
REHAB•TRANSFORMATION•REFORM

7 | PAROLED

Then you will know the truth, and the truth will set
you free.
John 8:32

My rapid exit from the meeting had come and gone. Now it was Wednesday night, another meeting night. Out of habit, I was getting ready to go, mind numb and my heart not inspired. But something had changed. I had not prepared for the meeting. This was a first for me.

As I got dressed, I caught my reflection in the mirror and said: "What are you doing? Why are you doing this to yourself?"

I threw my hands up in frustration and added: "God, if this means I'm going to die at Armageddon, then so be it. I can't do this anymore. I'm done."

I took off my meeting clothes, put on my comfortable pajamas, and turned the TV on. I felt nothing, no guilt. This moment offered me more peace than I had felt in a long time. Inexplicably, at that moment, all guilt, shame, and condemnation I had been carrying for so long just melted away.

Now, as always on Wednesday, my daughter also calls to see if I'm going to the meeting. My consistent attendance, I suspected, had started to put pressure on her to return to the kingdom hall. When I said "no," she asked if I was sick. I nonchalantly said: "No, I just don't feel like going." This was different from my usually cheerful tone of voice which exclaimed I was going to a meeting. I'd done this in the past—intentionally—because it seemed the best way to set an example of what I wanted her to do, not simply telling her. By going to the meetings, I had been showing Jehovah I wanted to restore my relationship with Him and serve Him with a clean conscience. This was how I believed Sophia would eventually follow suit.

My night was calm and stress free, and before long, I was ready for sleep. For the first time in a long time, my hand did not reach for my sleeping pills. When I laid my head down on my pillow, I drifted off to sleep. It was deep and beautiful. I slept like a baby that night for the first time in years.

I had told God a few hours earlier that He could kill me at Armageddon; I had made peace with death. And I was okay? Yes, I was alright!

There was no turning back. Other people's opinion of me leaving "the truth," was no longer relevant. My sanity was my priority now. The meeting the day after my birthday was my last meeting and I have not been back since. That was June of 2018.

Sophia kept checking on me every meeting night for the next two weeks until finally one day I decided it was time to let her know my decision. We arranged to meet for lunch.

"I'm not going back," I said.

"What do you mean?"

"I'm not getting reinstated and I'm not going back to the kingdom hall."

She was silent for a moment. I could see the wheels spinning in her head. What about Armageddon and paradise? What about everything I had taught her? Her mind seemed to drift off as if she was pondering if I was joking or if I knew what I was doing.

Then I said: "But I won't stop you from going back if that's what you want to do."

I shared with her how free I felt and how it felt like a burden was lifted. She realized I was very serious, and I could see a sense of relief come over her. She was caught off guard and didn't know what to say or what to ask me.

I also shared my decision with my brother Peter.

Strangely enough, he encouraged me to reconsider and urged me to go back so that I could connect with my family and friends again.

He said: "I don't think you want to do that."

"I can't do this any longer Peter. I'm done."

The struggle was unbearable and obviously, I did not fit in if it was taking me 50 years to get it right. Then he suggested I go back and "fade." Meaning, go inactive again. Which is where I was already before I went to the elders. I told him I couldn't do that either.

My brother is a family person and knows all too well the pain and struggles of going through life without his family and didn't want me to have the same experience.

We had been witnessing through him the harsh and cruel effects of disfellowshipping. The struggles he went through were not because he didn't have God's Holy Spirit, but because alienation from one's family is not normal, but inhumane.

My brother's experience was now teaching me. I knew I had to make a clean break, authentically—sever all ties. He was nervous for me because it took him way too long to recover from his traumatic experience with disfellowshipping. Peter had to learn to live without blood family and I had already been doing the same. I was just taking my next step. Yes, my mind was made up and there was nothing anyone could do to change it. This time it was a decision made with conviction, not a temporary emotion based on something stubborn brewing inside of me.

Once you are awake and see things for what they are, there is no turning back. I was centered enough to know I would not walk into the kingdom hall under false pretenses.

Let me be clear: I do not cast judgment on those who decide to stay and those who go back to preserve their family connections. Nor is it my place to judge them for making this excruciating choice. No one—and I mean no one—has the right to come between you and your family. This organization has destroyed the family structure, and many have gone to their graves without the parent/child bond being repaired. As for me, I still had Sophia and she is who I have had all along. My beautiful, loving, and supportive daughter.

I grew up being terrified of death and dying. My hope was always to be a person who just walked into paradise. Some people need to be resurrected to get in and some would never die—they just walk into the new world.

Look at me, I marveled. Awake and thinking about death, yet not afraid. And it felt good to experience this.

As I reflect on death, I think of going to funerals with my dad when I was young. The sight of dead people had always freaked me out. Knowing people could see my body, void of life, should I be in that casket one day and my mind somewhere else was unsettling. I was never able to reconcile this. Today, I no longer have a fear of death.

I did nothing for the next two months; no meeting, no studying, no Bible. Nothing! It was refreshing to detach from it all. But then I started to feel a void and wondered: *If what I just left is not the truth, then what is?*

During my time as a JW, I had on occasion watched Joel Osteen's program on TV. His messages had always been refreshing and motivating but left me feeling guilty at the same time.

The beliefs of my previous religion had pitted us against other religions. Other religions were false, and Jehovah's Witnesses were the one true religion chosen by Jesus and his Father to be His only organization on earth.

I had set my DVR to record and usually watched the program later in the day. One Sunday morning, I turned on the TV and watched it live. By now I was in the kitchen, cooking breakfast and doing a few other things. Before long the program ended, and a new one began.

I heard a voice I had never heard before. The voice was powerful, dynamic, and confident. His teaching style caught my attention. I stopped what I was doing and walked over to the TV to listen closer. It was Dr. Ed Young and the program was called The Winning Walk. I sat down and listened to the entire program. By the end of it, I was in tears.

I don't remember the subject matter, but it was so profound and deep—compelling and without guilt being projected. This is what I had been looking for. I was ready to learn "the meat" of the Bible, the deeper things. I was intrigued and wanted to hear more.

In the JW organization, this type of positive messaging is termed "tickling your ears," telling people what they wanted to hear and what sounded good.

But what I heard that day was completely different. My ears were not being tickled, but my heart was consumed with the message, and it was refreshing.

For many Sundays more I continued to listen. Every week my reaction was the same. The Winning Walk always ended with the message of developing a "closer relationship with Jesus." That's it. Just Jesus! There was no agenda, encouraging one to sacrifice their lives and dreams to do more for Jehovah by serving in the door-to-door work full time or serving at bethel. It is based simply on having a relationship with Jesus.

I was drawn to the simplicity of the message and I could no longer ignore my main thought: *Man, this sounds like the truth!*

Now I was even more awake.

What are "Other" Churches About?

Anything can sound good on TV. Maybe things were different off-camera. I decided it was time to hear the message in person. I looked up the church online and found a campus in my area and decided to go for it.

As I drove to the campus (which made me feel better than calling it a church) I was conflicted the entire fifteen minutes it took for me to get there. My mind was saying, *what are you doing, Gail?* But the car kept going.

I was about to walk into a church for worship, not a kingdom hall for the very first time in my life.

I pulled into the lot, parked the car, and spotted the sign on the building which read: Second Baptist Church Worship Center. An arrow pointed me in the direction of the auditorium.

I hung my head down so as not to see the sign. The rapid beat of my heart made me think it might jump right out of my chest. The fear of entering the building was real and intense.

Was I rebelling against God? Had Satan really gotten ahold of me and lured me into a church? More JW thoughts were echoing in my head. One who leaves Christendom, or Babylon the Great, the world empire of false religion, becomes a witness and then goes back to false religion, it is as if that person had returned to their own vomit, forgetting the things they have learned and turned their back on the things they have heard. Is that what I was doing?

I kept walking. Once inside the auditorium, I found a seat in the back. Soon after, a band came onto the stage and the music began. Right away, I smiled. I recognized the song from the radio. I had started listening to 89.3 KSBJ, a local Christian radio station. It is was beautiful hearing it live, and it brought me to tears. I was so moved.

When the song ended, we were encouraged to turn around and introduce ourselves to our neighbors. I was embarrassed because the tears were still running down my face and I had hoped that no one would notice.

Shortly after, the music began again, followed by a prayer and more music.

And then…

Whoa! What? The collection plate was passed…Was I finding a plus for JW's, a check one, so to speak? Not passing a collection plate had always been a source of pride for the organization, a statement they made in every publication. I must admit, that threw me for a loop, and I started to question if I really belonged there.

So much was happening, and another familiar song began. As a JW, it was a given that we did not listen to this type of music, as it originated from false religious teachings.

When the music ended it was time to hear the message, which I found out was only thirty minutes long. All in all, I was in and out in about one hour. I had managed it well and there was a lot to process.

I was grateful no one was checking on my attendance, there was no field service time to turn in, and participation was not dependent on me filling out a guest card.

Filling out the guest card was completely voluntary because the thought of anyone following up with me after this visit was not welcomed by me.

Despite the excitement I felt, it was too soon to let my guard down. I wasn't going to be bamboozled again. Therefore, I would remain an observer in the shadows. It felt good to slip in and out with no one asking if I was a member or not. I loved the anonymity and I could continue to be discreet during my investigation.

One thing that stood out at me was how refreshed I felt after leaving the service. What a difference! No feeling beat up or guilty for what I wasn't doing. Instead, I was filled with hope about what could possibly be. Freedom in Christ! A feeling I couldn't shake.

The music and the message had the same theme; Jesus. When I got home that day, I dropped to my knees and stated: *"God, I don't know who you are or who I have been praying to my entire life. Are you Jesus or Jehovah?"*

A passage from Matthew 11:28-30 began to resonate with me during this time: *"Come to me, all you who are weary and burdened, and I will give you rest. Take my yoke upon you and learn from me, for I am gentle and humble in heart, and you will find rest for your souls. For my yoke is easy and my burden is light."*

At this point, you may be thinking I had finally come across what I had been looking for all along. Everything was growing crystal clear. Nope. This was not the case. There was still a great deal of hesitation and I couldn't swat it away like a pesky fly.

I had figured, like with a relationship, leaving one bad one just to quickly enter another one is never a good idea. Leaving one religion with so much emotional trauma, to seek out another made me feel vulnerable to making a bad decision. It was a price I was not willing to pay. So, after six weeks, I stopped going and decided that it was possible to serve God at home without claiming a religion.

Another reason for this hesitation is because I committed to reading the entire Bible within the next year. I had promised myself this would be done before I made any life-changing decisions regarding my next move. I also justified that I should at least visit the two other churches I had on my list of possibilities (something I never did do).

So, I visited a local Christian bookstore to find a new Bible. There were so many to choose from that I must have been there for a couple of hours. Guess which Bible was not at the store? The New World Translation of the Holy Scriptures (NWT), translated by the Watchtower. This was the same time I realized how strange it was that the word Bible wasn't even in its title. Something I had never noticed.

After a couple of hours, I choose my Bible and checked out. As I was leaving the store, I noticed a scripture printed on the bag. It was John 14:6, the same scripture that woke me up. I was in disbelief at how intentional everything was coming together. I sat in my car with tears, just thanking God for leading me in the right direction.

For the following two months, I only read my Bible and watched The Winning Walk.

But...something was happening. I sensed a change in me, even in the prayers I prayed. They had become more heartfelt and I was talking to God. I craved this time with Him, as it was unbelievably special, so much so that I made a place in my tiny closet to talk to Him.

Learning the Bible became an obsession as I read more than 20 pages a day. It was as intriguing as learning a new language in a foreign country. But I loved it.

As I craved more knowledge, I found my research to be enjoyable—eye-opening. I soaked everything up like a sponge. This ultimately became part of the healing process that brought me peace of mind. I realized how spiritually malnourished I had been.

Growing up, I had been taught that learning the Bible without the aid of the Watchtower publications was just not possible. Now I was learning on my own that I could get to know God better, without the indoctrination of a system. This was incredibly liberating. It opened my heart and mind to examine that which would have otherwise gone undiscovered.

2 Timothy 3:7 describes perfectly my life as a JW: *"...always learning but never able to come to a knowledge of the truth."*

The Watchtower Society was enthusiastic to inundate its members with an abundance of material. Even for the most devout, it was an impossible pace to keep up with; however, it did serve a beneficial purpose to the organization. Witnesses are presented with new releases at regional conventions and it was always an exciting time for a JW. Research publications were presented under the premise that they had done all the research for us; and because the trust factor was already in place, there was no need to go looking for the information ourselves, especially on the internet. There was so much information, we had become lazy and dependent on the spiritual food they were providing.

Researching and spiritually nourishing myself proved to be satisfying.

As for what I began to feel about Watchtower's methods, I am still coming to terms with the gravity of the potential deception. I'm still not ready to make the conclusion that it was deliberate. What I know to be true is that I felt more liberated as the chains came off.

Something else that jolted me was information I found while researching the internet. I came across the Australian Royal Commission that was formed to investigate how institutions like schools, churches, sports clubs, and governmental organizations have responded to allegations of child sexual abuse.

The Jehovah's Witnesses were investigated under Case Study 29 because of their lack of reporting allegations of child sexual abuse to the authorities. That is where I found out the elders write a report to the Society of the judicial committee meeting and the results on a form called S-77. I was horrified because in all my years I had never known about this. In addition, why did they keep a record of my sins or anything else? I started to wonder what was on this report and the report from the previous three hearings.

Learning what I had, I felt horrified. This is when my gloves officially came off, and I felt ready to take on Watchtower. For starters, I reached out to my attorney, who wrote a nice letter demanding my records

Here is a copy of the 1-page letter she wrote (file # redacted).

LAW OFFICES
R~~O~~S~~S~~ & ~~MATTHEWS~~, P.C.
Fort Worth, Texas 76~~~~

Phone (817) 255-2044
Please reference our File Number ████ when replying

Fax (817) 255-2090
Mary G. Eads, of Counsel

June 18, 2018

Watchtower Bible & Tract Society
Attn.: Legal Department/Administrative Offices/
Services Department
1 Kings Drive
Tuxedo Park, NY 10987

CERTIFIED MAIL NO.: 9171 9690 0935 0202 1300 76
RETURN RECEIPT REQUESTED
AND U.S. FIRST CLASS MAIL

Re: *Gail T. Appling formerly known as Gail T. White*

Dear Sir or Madam:

This letter is written on behalf of Gail T. Appling. Ms. Appling has advised me that on September 28, 2017, she requested a copy of her file via telephone from someone in the Watchtower Bible & Tract Society Service Department. As of this date, the file has not been provided.

The purpose of this letter is to demand that a copy of the entire file be forwarded to me. Please include unredacted documentation in your possession on Gail T. Appling, formerly Gail T. White, from June 1986 through the current date. This includes, without limitation, any documents in electronic or paper form dealing with disciplinary actions that may have been taken against her, whether those actions constituted private reproof or other actions up to and including disfellowshipping. Also to be included are any notes related to Shepherding calls and correspondence between the main Watchtower office and Ms. Appling's circuit and district overseers and local bodies of elders with the various congregations with which she has been associated.

Please forward the documents to the undersigned. If I have not received these documents within thirty (30) days of your receipt of this letter, I will have no alternative but to recommend that Ms. Appling take further legal action to obtain copies of her file.

Yours very truly,

Mary G. Eads,
Of Counsel

MGE/bc
cc: Gail T. Appling
Intake No.: ████

Just to be clear, I had no expectation of receiving a response. But to my surprise, they did respond to my attorney with a 2-page letter.

┌┐┌┐┌┐

WATCHTOWER
Bible and Tract Society of New York, Inc.
Legal Department
100 Watchtower Drive, Patterson, NY 12563-9204, U.S.A.
Phone: (845) 306-1000   Fax: (845) 306-0709

July 2, 2018

Mary G. Eads, Esq.
Ross & Matthews, P.C.
3650 Lovell Avenue
Fort Worth, Texas 76107

Re: Gail T. Appling-Formerly Known as Gail T. White

Dear Ms. Eads:

Your letter of June 18, 2018, was referred to me to respond. You demand a copy of "the entire file" concerning your client, Gail T. Appling. Watchtower has no file on your client to provide and we would not provide it if we had one. The Service Department of the United States Branch Office of Jehovah's Witnesses has only an electronic notation showing that Gail T. Appling is no longer one of Jehovah's Witnesses because she was disfellowshipped in October 2017. If and when she is reinstated as one of Jehovah's Witnesses the Service Department will delete that notation.

The decision to disfellowship is a spiritual one, based entirely upon the Bible. Unlike other religions, a disfellowshipping in the faith of Jehovah's Witnesses is not permanent. One who has been disfellowshipped may request reinstatement.

There is no legal recourse to the religious decision of elders in congregations of Jehovah's Witnesses to disfellowship. Others have filed suit over having been disfellowshipped and the decisions of the courts have uniformly upheld the right of religions to discipline their members. You may wish to review the line of cases decided by courts in Tennessee beginning with *Travers v. Abbey*, 58 S.W.247 (Tenn 1900) and including *Mason v. Winstead*, 265 S.W.2d 561 (Tenn 1954) and *Anderson v. Watchtower Bible and Tract Society of New York, Inc.*, 2007 WL 161035 (Tenn.Ct.App.), as well as cases from other jurisdictions such as *Paul v. Watchtower Bible & Tract Soc'y of New York, Inc.*, 819 F.2d 875 (9th Cir. 1987), *Rasmussen v. Bennett*, 741 P.2d 755 (Mont. 1987); *Abrams v. Watchtower Bible & Tract Soc'y of New York, Inc.*, 715 N.E.2d 798 (Ill.App.Ct. 1999); *Presbyterian Church v. Mary E.B. Hull Mem'l Pres. Church*, 393 U.S. 440 (1969), and the line of cases that include *Gonzalez v. Roman Catholic Archbishop*, 280 U.S. 1, 50 S.Ct. 5 (1929); *Kedroff v. St. Nicholas Cathedral*, 344 U.S. 94, 73 S.Ct. 143 (1952); *Presbyterian Church v Mary Elizabeth Hull Memorial Presbyterian Church*, 393 U.S. 440, 89 S.Ct. 601 (1969), and *Serbian Eastern Orthodox Diocese v. Milivojevich*, 426 U.S. 696, 96 S.Ct. 2372 (1976) dealing with the ecclesiastical abstention doctrine.

129

In *Watson v. Jones*, 80 U.S. 679, 13 Wall 679, 20 L.Ed 666 (1871) the United States Supreme Court listed some examples of matters over which courts have no jurisdiction that are entirely within the authority of the church body to decide. They include "the conformity of the members of the church to the standard of morals required of them." *Id.* at 733. The Court refused to allow civil or secular courts to hear attacks on a church tribunal decision concerning membership. *Id.* at 733-34.

Glass v. First United Pentecostal Church of DeRidder, 676 S.2d 724 (La.App. 1966) is another example of a court ruling that courts have no jurisdiction over expulsion from church. See also *Crosby v. Lee*, 76 S.E. 2d 856 (Ga.App. 1953); *Fowler v. Bailey*, 844 P.2d 141 (Okla 1992); and *Grunwald v. Bornfreund*, 696 F.Supp. 838 (E.D.N.Y. 1988).

In Texas, the decisions in *Tilton v. Marshall*, 925 S.W.2d 672 (1996) and *Westbrook v. Penley*, 231 S.W.3d 389 (2007) provide guidance that help explain our position. *Tilton* discusses discovery of church documents and *Westbrook* discusses the constitutionality of courts weighing in on church discipline. Elders in the faith of Jehovah's Witnesses confine themselves to providing Scriptural counsel and administering internal church discipline. Thus, there is no deviation from one's role as spiritual counselor, as occurred in *Westbrook*.

Again, your client is free to avail herself of the opportunity to seek reinstatement as one of Jehovah's Witnesses.

If you would like to discuss the matter further, please feel free to call me.

Sincerely,

John O. Miller III
Associate General Counsel

JOM:rle

Although I didn't get what I asked for, I got what I had expected; their evasive response in bold print.

My attorney could write a letter to Watchtower because they are a corporation. I wanted her to write a letter to the local body of elders, but she could not because of the church-state separation. So, I wrote one myself. Here is a copy of the 2-page (also redacted) letter I sent them.

130

Gail T. Appling

July 5, 2018

Mr.

Mr.

Mr.

Re: Breach of Confidence and Abusive Process
        Judicial Committee Meeting for Gail Appling

Gentlemen:

As you are aware, I attended a Judicial Committee hearing on September 27, 2017. At the commencement of this meeting, I was assured confidentiality. The context of the meeting was extremely uncomfortable in that you three gentlemen were in close proximity to me in a locked room. Although you may have thought that this created a sense of closeness, in fact, it came across as a situation suggesting an imbalance of power. It would have been far more appropriate for us to be seated at a table where I could have felt that I had some personal space and I was not being bullied.

In the weeks that followed the committee meeting, despite the pledge of confidentiality, I heard details I communicated to you in that meeting in confidence referred to from the stage to the audience of the Southlake Houston Congregation. In addition, during the week of the visit of the Circuit Overseer, Lee Smith, he too gave details from information discussed in the meeting, even in prayer. I perceive this serious breach of confidentiality as an egregious betrayal of trust.

Under the guise of "ministering" to me, you exploited the confidences shared with you. In my opinion this is an abuse of power and constitutes psychological and spiritual abuse.

Despite having gone through the five-hour long Judicial Committee Process, and having attended meetings for months following the Committee Meeting in which I was shunned, you have presumed to judge me as "unrepentant". I am convinced that your claim to understanding what is in my heart is wrong.

131

Your inappropriate actions have taken away what might otherwise have been the church's sustaining spiritual guidance and support. Although some report that after an experience such as mine, their trust has been so violated that they can no longer attend any church, I take comfort in the fact that my trust in the Lord sustains me.

Cordially,

Gail T. Appling

CC: Lee Smith, Circuit Overseer
█████████████████

Via certified mail: 7017 2400 0001 0652 7042

Watchtower Bible & Tract Society
c/o Legal Department, Administrative Offices & Service Department
1 Kings Drive
Tuxedo Park, NY 10987
Via certified mail: 7017 2400 0001 0652 7059

All the letters were sent certified, so I have proof they got it. Naturally, there was no response to my letter to the judicial committee; however, these letters are of great value to me. They signify me taking back my power, letting them know I no longer recognized their authority over me and that there was nothing they could do about it.

It felt good to have my power back and by tapping into it, I was no longer afraid.

"The Lord is with me; I will not be afraid. What can mere mortals do to me?"-Psalm 118:6.

That's all they were, mortals; subject to death just like me.

I was finally paroled.

8 | CASE CLOSED

Be alert and of sober mind. Your enemy the devil prowls around like a roaring lion looking for someone to devour.

1 Peter 5:8

With each passing day, my faith in God had grown stronger. I began learning so much just by reading the Bible and listening to sermons than I had been taught the previous fifty years.

Everything was on track, right? Well, it was looking good, but I would have been naïve to think the devil would let me go easily.

When I neared the one-year mark since the disfellowshipping announcement, October 2018, people were expecting the announcement for my reinstatement any day. Knowing this, I decided to write my parents a letter to let them know my decision to not return to the organization.

I typed the letter up and dropped it at my dad's front door, also attaching a copy of the correspondence I'd had with Watchtower. I mailed a copy to my mom, who lives out of state.

After I drove off from his house, I got a call from my brother, Abraham, letting me know Dad was sick, and it was serious. Of course, I felt bad.

So, the next day, I went back, hoping I would be able to see him. This was an emergency, which meant it surely constituted an exception for communication.

I knocked on the front door. His wife opened the door and without saying a word, allowed me to enter the house and pointed to his office.

I walked in and there I was, face-to-face with Dad. I asked him what was going on with his health. We talked about that for about twenty minutes before he finally got around to asking what my letter was about.

"Did you read it?" I asked. He said he read some of it. I did notice the letter was nowhere in sight. Had he tossed it out?

My previous teachings guided me to the hesitation I was experiencing. With me being disfellowshipped, in the mind of a JW, it is inconceivable for me to be quoting scripture since the actions taken against me had deemed me to be spiritually weak in faith. So, to open a letter and see scriptural references meant only one other thing: I must be sharing apostate information and my intentions are to be questioned.

JW's are trained to view anything that does not originate with Watchtower as false and should be avoided like poison. Witnesses are cautioned about the media and watching anything that speaks about Jehovah's Witnesses in a negative light and to immediately destroy and discard anything that looks apostate. They refer to it as "hearsay and apostate driven lies to separate one from Jehovah." This fear-based message is in most everything. Because of this, most never investigate for themselves.

My dad's nonchalant approach to the letter did not surprise me, but I wondered how he could read the letter and not be moved. My letter was void of opinion and was based entirely on scripture and the new things I had learned.

Then he asked the question every JW asks due to feeling they have the truth and everything else is false: "Where are you going to go then?"

I'm not sure what made me say this, but I said: "I am in the Body of Christ."

"That's what all apostates say." This was his response.

JWs are trained to have this knee jerk reaction to expressions that have never been used in the Watchtower publications. They teach that apostates have an independent spirit and are possibly "mentally diseased" as they seek to sow doubts to draw the "sheep" away from the congregation.

The Watchtower article, "Will You Heed Jehovah's Clear Warnings?" July 14, 2011, pp. 15-19, states: "Apostates are mentally diseased. They seek to infect others with their disloyal teachings."

Being labeled an "apostate" is very demeaning, defamatory and ruins one's reputation and good name. Apostates are equated to Satan, which makes this libelous slander.

Consider this statement from the Watchtower article, "Job Held High the Name of Jehovah," April 15, 2009, par. 15.

15. What do modern-day apostates have in common with Satan?

[15] Satan was the first creature to turn apostate. Modern-day apostates display characteristics similar to those of the Devil. Their mind may be poisoned by a critical

attitude toward individuals in the congregations, Christian elders, or the Governing Body. Some apostates oppose the use of the divine name, Jehovah. They are not interested in learning about Jehovah or in serving him. Like their father, Satan, apostates target people of integrity. (John 8:44) No wonder servants of Jehovah avoid all contact with them!—2 John 10, 11.

It's meaning is relatively simple. An apostate is "a person who renounces a religious or political belief or principle (Oxford Dictionary)". It is the fallout which is associated with this label that shows just how vindictive the JW machine is. If they can no longer control you, they control the way others see you, by using the silent treatment, name-calling, or labeling.

Yet, I had just confessed my faith in Jesus, and he thinks that I am an apostate, at least according to Watchtowers definition. There was some serious cognitive dissonance going on.

Another thing my dad said was that my actions showed I didn't recognize the elders as God appointed. The same spirit that appointed them can take them out, but I hadn't given Jehovah a chance to do that. I decided to do it on my own. He continues talking about how disfellowshipping was just a temporary thing.

His reaction was not uncommon since the focus is always on Jehovah. If you profess your faith in Jesus as your Lord and Savior to a witness, you are likely to be corrected and told it is Jehovah.

Then, I brought up the serious issue of suicide that shunning has caused in the life of others, which Watchtower never talks about. I shared how my experience taught me how wrong disfellowshipping was and wondered how many people I had shunned unjustly.

I felt it best to avoid the other hot topic that has gained attention in the news lately, namely, the serious allegations of alleged child sexual abuse cover-up, feeling I had a better chance of connecting through a non-controversial topic.

Then I asked a provocative question. "If I had gone through with taking my life; how would you be feeling right now?"

He answered that he'd be hurt, just as me leaving the organization hurt.

I understood why he said it, especially since he was also an elder, but it was still painful. It served as further evidence of how the teachings of JW rob a person of their natural affection. In the last days, people will have no natural affection. In the NWT version, 2 Timothy 3:3 reads: "having no natural affection, not open to any agreement, slanderers, without self-control, fierce, without love of goodness." I was witnessing this firsthand through my father.

Implicit trust in the elders was his driving force and something his position required him to uphold. Again, elders being guided by the Holy Spirit were the source of information, not him, personally. He still trusted the disfellowshipping decision as being the correct one.

I also mentioned how I learned that some people go back to the organization only to get their friends and family. He acknowledged the elders were aware of this and were on guard against those who would try to be deceitful with their words or emotions. In other words, it's harder to get reinstated now.

"Who are you to judge and who are you to keep people from their family?" I asked this with a sickened heart, finding it hard to see my dad, someone I loved, being so detached to the suffering of others. I didn't recognize this person.

"Why are people being forced to 'work the system,' so to speak? Take them at their word, let them come back and leave the rest to God. End of story."

The conversation lasted for about an hour and twenty minutes. Then I left, not sure what else there was to say, but also surprised he had accommodated me for so long. His parting words were ones filled with hopefulness. He suggested I think about what I was doing and hurry up and come back soon because Armageddon was just around the corner.

This was on a Monday and by the following Sunday I learned my dad was in the hospital; he had been since Thursday.

No one called me. Not his wife, not his congregation.

As soon as Abraham found out, he called me and told me what hospital he was in. I didn't know what would happen, but I was going to go see him.

Later that day, I stood outside his room and took a deep breath and then entered.

Dad looked worse than he had when I'd seen him just six days ago. The change was drastic, and my heart sunk.

He was always a slight man and had lost about twenty pounds. But he had enough strength to resist me as I tried to find out how he was doing and understand what was going on with his health.

He answered my questions vaguely, if it all.

His body language made it obvious he did not want me there.

Watchtower would be proud.

I planned on sticking it out, though. We were in a public setting and he could not kick me out.

Finally, he asked what my decision was (regarding being reinstated as a JW).

I reminded him that I had already shared my decision in the letter I delivered a week ago and during the discussion at his home. My purpose for being at the hospital with him was to see about his wellbeing.

He then said: "If that is your final decision…" His words faded away and fragments about being loyal to Jehovah came out of his mouth and a few other things. Eventually, he asked me what the scripture at 2 John 9-11 said. I said I didn't know, but I would look it up when I got home. I later discovered it was the popular scripture Watchtower refers to regarding how to view and treat apostates. The NWT version reads:

> "Everyone who pushes ahead and does not remain in the teaching of the Christ does not have God. The one who

does remain in this teaching is the one who has both the Father and the Son. If anyone comes to you and does not bring this teaching, do not receive him into your homes or say a greeting to him. For the one who says a greeting to him is a sharer in his wicked works."

There it is. Anyone who leaves "the truth" is "wicked" and not waiting on Jehovah but running ahead with their own teachings.

Being a researcher of all things related to my former belief in comparison to the truth now, I found it very interesting to learn why Paul said this. Paul said that because there were Christians who did not believe in the deity of Jesus.

Furthermore, my extensive research solidified in my mind that Jehovah's Witnesses may be the apostates. The governing body have put a layer of communication between the members and God, making themselves mediators. Everyone can have a direct relationship with Jesus Christ, who is the bridge to the Father.

When I reflected on the visit to the hospital room, I felt hurt about my dad trying so hard to avoid speaking to me and his spiritual discipline. I felt like he was strong-arming me to come back.

Disfellowshipping is a weapon the Watchtower society uses as its shield against people leaving the organization. It is tantamount to emotional blackmail, and its members unwittingly go along with it.

We had built a business together and worked together for so many years. This meant nothing to him, I guess.

His struggle with my presence was eased by a few witnesses entering the room to visit him. He brightened up and warmly welcomed them. That was my cue to leave and I did.

Tears welled up in my eyes. It stung deeply, but I would not be shaken. I would not change my mind. I was firm in my decision. You see, Jesus left the ninety-nine and came and got me. I couldn't and I won't turn my back on that kind of love.

In a time when I needed much love and support, their solution was to expel me from the congregation. I was discarded, thrown into a pit, left on the side of the road for dead, as it were.

But I found a new beginning and there was no human relationship that could compare to the peace and love I now have and feel daily. No one can take that away from me and this is something I will not give up.

That night I tossed and turned, and I couldn't sleep. It bothered me to see the stronghold the organization had on my dad's natural affections.

These intense emotions carried on through the next day and I wrestled with them in silence. My daughter had been through enough and heard enough. Not knowing to whom or where I could turn, I decided to go online and fill out a prayer request.

Moments of weakness surfaced, and I began to ask if this is what it was going to take for me to give in, change my mind and get reinstated; to be able to reconnect with my dad and family again?

Then my imagination started to run wild. I thought about going to the next meeting, to let the elders know that my dad was very ill, that things weren't looking good for him and demand they reinstate me that night. (In my mind, it looked more like a bum rush. Ha!) The question I would put forth to them was, could they live with themselves if he passed away?

The bigger question, however, was, could **I** live with myself if he did?

My decision was clearly being put to the test.

I had reached my breaking point.

Then, a few hours later, I received a phone call from the daughter of the friend I called the night of the announcement. She had four children who were not witnesses. I had seen them on occasion when I went to visit their mother and always wanted to get to know them. But there was this Watchtower gap between us. They didn't know if I would try to talk them into coming back to the organization.

So, imagine my surprise when Valencia's name popped up on my caller ID. I gathered myself and answered the phone and she said she was checking on me. She said her mother missed me, and that she had been listening for my name to be announced any day now. I missed her mother too, and then shared with her that I wouldn't be returning. The problem was, with my dad in the hospital I felt like I was being coerced into going back against my will.

She was surprised to hear I was not going back, yet happy to know I was free.

The next day I got a text from her with a message from all her siblings saying that they were praying for me and to hang in there. This interaction lifted my spirits and strengthened me to keep going. I didn't feel so isolated anymore and felt visible for the first time in a long time. God works in mysterious ways and He used Valencia to answer my prayer request that day. I thank her often for answering God's call because that call was a turning point for me.

Sometime later, a woman named Monica, from Arizona called in response to the prayer request I had submitted online. I had been so distraught at the time I couldn't remember what I had written down.

Where this conversation gets fascinating is this woman who called to pray with me, was herself a former JW.

WOW! Look at God! The emotions welled up inside of me and I was astounded at how only He could have orchestrated all of this. None of it had been a coincidence.

She shared her experience with me, and I felt strengthened even more. She said I could call her any time, and now I had a new friend in another state.

Not long after this, I ran across a couple in the area where I live and had known from my time in the organization. I had seen Sharon at the store one day and avoided her because I just did not feel like telling one more person that I was disfellowshipped. Later, quite by chance, I found out that she and her husband, Rob, had left the organization a few years back. So I reached out to them.

We met at a café and spent about four hours just talking. They were so encouraging, sharing insights about what they had learned. It became an impromptu Bible study.

Just like that, in a short space of time, God had connected me with people to let me know I was not alone. They were out there. People who not only understood what I was going through and could help me move past it, but also helped me reveal the beauty of my future. God was strengthening me, sending people who showed unconditional love. There was hope.

Through these new connections, He answered my lingering question, showing me through my new friends, that I would be all right and life outside of Watchtower was possible.

Nothing "bad" happened to these people because they left the organization. And while they were not immune to life's daily struggles, they were making it in a non-JW world.

Everything I had experienced over the past year, brought back to my memory a situation that happened when I was just twelve-years-old living in Brooklyn, New York. It was 1980, and many Bethelites (those who serve at headquarters voluntarily) were being disfellowshipped. Some attended the congregation our family attended. I remembered going to my best friend's house to prepare for the Watchtower study with other friends. We were asked to stop having these small study groups and I later learned that some witnesses among us were spreading false teachings. It was a very interesting time, as they were accused of being rebellious ones who wanted to create division and start their own sects; Apostates!

Recently I found out that one of the individuals who was disfellowshipped, Raymond Franz, a former member of the governing body, had written a book called *Crisis of Conscience*. I was infuriated to learn the truth behind this upheaval at Bethel and that we had been lied to. If they lied to us about that, what else had they lied about? I was devastated for thinking ill of this man for so many years and realizing how much of my life was wasted in this organization. What makes Franz' book very powerful is that as a researcher for the organization, charged with writing much of the literature like what I have discussed, realized this organization was not teaching the truth. That "we were not the advanced Bible scholars we thought we were (Crisis of Conscience)". I felt the same way when I started studying the Bible without the lens of the Watchtower publications.

Franz passed away in 2010 at the age of eighty-eight. His book woke up a lot of people then and it still does today— for those Jehovah's Witnesses who read it for themselves.

It takes courage to pick up a book like that and question your faith, especially when you are conditioned to think the information you learn in the publications is coming directly from Jehovah, through Jesus, and down to the governing body, God's channel of communication.

Ray and the others were condemned through harsh words and slander. However, the stand they took for the truth is at play today, setting many people free and saving many lives.

Increasing questions and challenges being presented to headquarters have led to a new wave of disfellowshipping in the Watchtower organization. Over time, the teachings in the organization have been adjusted. It is referred to as "new light" or "beliefs clarified." This is how the organization explains variations to previous teachings and that the truth is being progressively revealed over time.

One of the biggest questions being asked is regarding the failed prophecies.

Failed prophecies are a hot topic for many who have believed with their whole heart they would not grow old in this system, that they didn't need to go to college or saw it as best to defer their hopes and dreams for full-time service. The teaching that the generation who was alive during 1914 would not pass away before the end came, has been a big flop. That generation has died off and we are all still here. The new teaching now is "overlapping generations." Don't ask me how to explain that one.

The internet has changed all of this because even though it is discouraged, it is still used to some extent. The governing body has admitted they are "neither inspired nor infallible." They also say they "can err in doctrinal matters or in organizational direction." (Taken from Watchtower, "Who Is Leading God's People Today?" February 2017, paragraph 12.) Yet, if someone questions the teachings, they run the risk of being disfellowshipped, separated from family and friends, until they repent and comply.

At one time, most could not handle the rejection and returned to the organization. However, many are beginning to stand up to this ruthless organization and have refused to give in to their emotional blackmail.

But James 1:16, 17 says:

> *"Don't be deceived, my dear brothers and sisters. Every good and perfect gift is from above, coming down from the Father of the heavenly lights, who does not change like shifting shadows."*

There it is! God does not change. He is the same yesterday, today, and forever. So, why are the teachings constantly changing? For a God who never changes, the teachings of the Watchtower change constantly.

As all these deceptions were uncovered, I started to feel stronger and more at peace about my decision to not go back to the JW world.

Still, I was struggling and conflicted inside. One of my initial fears of leaving the organization was regarding who would check on me in case of an emergency. During hurricanes or tropical storms, I would usually get a call or text from the brothers asking if I was okay or needed any help. During Hurricane Harvey, sadly, many of the witnesses lost their homes. But it was truly heartwarming to see the friends risking their lives to rescue those who were trapped, opening their homes and assisting with the clean-up and rebuilding work.

I was fortunate that my home didn't flood. But who knew what the next storm would bring? With the unpredictable weather pattern, chances are eventually it would flood in my area. So, the lonely feeling of having no one to check on me was intimidating.

Still, I was willing to take my chances.

Not too long after, there was bad weather again, a tropical storm. Another flood came along with it. The same people were flooded, plus areas that did not flood during the earlier hurricane were now flooded. It was devastating!

During the storm, I got a text message from my group at church asking if everyone was okay. If anyone needed help, they would send out our address and as soon as the storm passed, they would be happy to come and help.

My rational fear and doubts were lifted, and this text message let me know that the church had a system in place to do the very thing I was afraid of not having. There are people that are concerned about their members—and their community. JWs typically only help JWs, whereas my new church helps as many in need as they can.

As relief and awareness grew in strength, the more open I became to an ever-improving belief system. I was at peace and it feels so good!

Case closed.

9 | THE LAW OF GRACE EXONERATES

"I do not set aside the grace of God, for if righteousness could be gained through the law, Christ died for nothing!"

Galatians 2:21

Many outsiders looking into the Watchtower organization, often wondered how Jehovah's Witnesses could not see what they saw so clearly. Was it a lack of intelligence? Once upon a time I brushed these voices off; only now am I beginning to wonder how I could have been fooled.

Witnesses are taught that you cannot understand the Bible without their publications, which I now know is false. I have experienced the Holy Spirit helping me understand the things I read. And what I read opened my eyes.

All of this is not as complicated as I was once led to believe. I have found ways to learn and grow in both knowledge and faith.

One way I have learned God's Word and about Jesus' role in my life is through music. There are many messages to take away from songs, as many of them are rooted in biblical passages and scripture. These beautiful melodies have offered me strength and hope when things got tough and I felt continually challenged by my past beliefs.

One of the first songs I heard when I started listening to Christian radio was *The Way* by Pat Barrett, a song based on John 14:6, the scripture that woke me up. That song still brings tears to my eyes.

Another song that helped me tremendously is called *Glorious Day* by Casting Crowns. Some of the words include "living He loved me," "dying He saved me," "buried He carried my sins far away," and "rising He justified, freely forever, one day He is coming, oh glorious day." Wow! My appreciation for what Jesus has done for me grows every time I hear this song.

So why was I crucified? This is what disfellowshipping feels like. Like carrying the weight of your sin, shame, embarrassment, and humiliation on an already beaten down soul. Why had I been made to go through such a burden if Jesus had already done it for me?

Another favorite song for me is *Grace Got You* by MercyMe. The song had a catchy upbeat tone to it, and I would hear the same song every time I got in my car. This happened often. I am fascinated by how God speaks.

As I listened closer, I thought, *hmm*? *Grace*? *I don't recall learning about grace.* I was familiar with the song *Amazing Grace*, but I had never had an interest in listening to it. This was a foreign concept to me, and I started to wonder what "grace" was.

I was compelled to find out more. I went home and googled "grace" to find out what scriptures in the Bible used that word. I cross-referenced the scriptures to the New World Translation and found out grace had been replaced—yes replaced—with the phrase "undeserved kindness." That was the term I was familiar with; I'd heard it my entire life but never made the connection of that phrase to the word grace.

To give you an idea of how different this looks in context let's consider a couple of verses.

John 1:16 in the NIV says:

> *"Out of his fullness we have all received grace in place of grace already given."*

John 1:16 in the NWT says:

> "For we all received from his fullness, even undeserved kindness upon undeserved kindness."

Romans 3:24 in the NIV says:

> *"and all are justified freely by his grace through the redemption that came by Christ Jesus."*

Romans 3:24 in the NWT says:

> "and it is as a free gift that they are being declared righteous by his undeserved kindness through the release by the ransom paid by Christ Jesus."

So which Bible translation is correct and how would I find out? To me, it appeared that the term "undeserved kindness" altered how the concept of grace could be viewed and applied to life.

With the assistance of websites like www.BibleStudyTools.com and www.PreceptAustin.org, I was able to find most of the scriptures that used the word "grace." I made a spreadsheet of all the scriptures, more than 165 of them.

I had both bibles opened, the New World Translation and The New International Version.

I remembered in our family library there was a purple book called *The Kingdom Interlinear Translation of the Greek Scriptures,* published by Watchtower, 1969. That would have been useful in my search but my chances of ever getting my mother to send it to me were nonexistent. I did a google search for "Greek interlinear" and the website www.scripture4all.org popped up. This site shows the original Greek word and its translation.

In time, I did find a copy of the *Kingdom Interlinear* on eBay, which helps me with my studies.

Now, let's go deeper into my investigation.

I read all 165+ scriptures from all three Bibles.

The original Greek words *kharis, kharin,* or *kharitoo,* is rendered as "grace." It is also where we get the words charity and charisma.

At times, the word "gift" is used in place of grace; however, it is still the same base word in the original Greek.

In the NWT, the word "grace" is used ZERO TIMES. The most popular phrase they replace grace with is "undeserved kindness," which is used 138 times out of 165 uses in other translation. Words such as gift, favor, credit, and gracious make up the remaining 27. By comparison, in the NIV version, the word "grace" is replaced 42 times, using words such as favor, blessing, the privilege of sharing, and thanksgiving, plus a few others to make up the difference.

Through what I've sought out for valid information, I know this:

- There is a deep deception going on.
- Words were changed to match the Watchtower theology. The question is, Why?

Consider this quote from the study article, "Grateful Recipients of God's Undeserved Kindness", Watchtower (Study Edition), July 2016, pp. 21-25.

> Regarding the word for "undeserved kindness," which is translated "grace" in many Bible versions, one scholar wrote: "The whole basic idea of the word is that of a free and undeserved gift, of something given to a man unearned and unmerited."

But later in the article, "undeserved kindness" is connected to works. Here's how:

> **18.** Because of Jehovah's undeserved kindness, what responsibilities do we have?
>
> [18] As grateful recipients of Jehovah's kindness, we owe it to him and to our neighbor to use our gifts to honor God and benefit our fellow man. In what ways? Paul answers: "Since, then, we have gifts that differ according to the undeserved kindness given to us . . . if it is a ministry, let us be at this ministry; or the one who teaches, let him be at his teaching; or the one who encourages, let him give encouragement; . . . the one who shows mercy, let him do it cheerfully." (Rom. 12:6-8) The undeserved kindness that Jehovah extends to us puts us under obligation to busy ourselves in the Christian ministry, to teach the Bible to others, to encourage fellow Christians, and to forgive any who may offend us.

19. What responsibility of ours will be examined in the next article?

[19] As grateful recipients of God's generous love, we should be moved to do our utmost "to bear thorough witness to the good news of the undeserved kindness of God." (Acts 20:24)

I found other instances where words are changed to promote the Watchtower theology; therefore, hiding the true meaning of the scripture.

With this revelation, I became passionate about learning the Word of God, which meant looking at the original Greek language, exploring different versions of the Bible, then comparing them against the NWT I was raised on.

Another discrepancy which alters the meaning of the scriptures is the word for "believe."

Romans 10:9 in the NIV says:

> *"If you declare with your mouth, "Jesus is Lord," and believe in your heart that God raised him from the dead, you will be saved."*

Romans 10:9[1] in the NWT says:

> "For if you publicly declare with your mouth that Jesus is Lord, and exercise faith in your heart that God raised him up from the dead, you will be saved."

---

[1] Romans 10:9 and 10:13 contradict in NWT. I encourage you to research it with the same resources mentioned above and see if you can find it.

The Greek word *pisteuo* means to believe or have faith. All other translations agree. In some cases, the NWT used the term *"exercise faith."*

Changing the word from "believe" to "exercise faith" denotes action and motivates a person to put forth works. Consider the article in Watchtower (Study Edition), "Exercise Your Faith in Jehovah's Promises", October 2016, paragraph 4:

> Faith involves much more than a mental understanding of God's purpose. It is a powerful motivating force that impels a person to act in harmony with God's will. Faith in God's means of salvation moves a believer to share the good news with others.

While that statement is not entirely false, that belief in God would motivate a person to tell others about Him, all Jehovah's Witnesses know the inference of this paragraph is to their primary purpose; the preaching work, the placing of literature, starting Bible studies, and reporting the amount of time spent in the ministry.

There are enough discrepancies to alter what seems to be the true Word of God. I hope this paints a clearer picture of why Jehovah's Witnesses believe the way they do.

It is heartbreaking how the Watchtower went to such great lengths to obscure the meaning of grace. These are no minor changes.

I also wonder, if Jehovah's Witnesses understood that grace was available to all, would they also understand the freedom that comes from believing in Christ?

My journey into understanding the Bible continues and it has taught me much, as well as helped me realize how much more I crave to know.

One thing is for certain: Jesus came for sinners, not saints. Luke 5:32 says: *"I have not come to call the righteous, but sinners to repentance."* In Mark 2:17, he said: *"I have not come to call the righteous, but sinners."* Everyone Jesus encountered was healed and became believers. He never turned anyone away nor did He ostracize them. Not the Samaritan woman at Jacob's well, not the woman in the synagogue spoken about at John 8:1-11. To the best of my knowledge, the experience of the woman who was caught in the act of adultery is one that has never been discussed in the Watchtower publications. I encourage you to read the full passage for yourself in the NWT to gain a full perspective. When I did this, reading the passage was not only new to me, but it showed me the heart of Jesus; the compassion, empathy, and love He had for people. He told the woman to "Go now and leave your life of sin." Contrast the way He dealt with her against the Pharisees who wanted to stone her; Jesus showed her grace.

The only people Jesus rebuked were the Pharisees and Sadducees, who insisted on living under the law, adding to it, and burdening the people with their endless rules and regulations.

Jesus had already done the work when He was crucified. He said: "It is finished." The blood of Jesus' sacrifice set us free from the law 2,000 years ago.

The tug of war between law and grace continued well after Jesus died; and through the pages of this book, it is evident that it continues today.

A common theme in the letters the apostle Paul wrote warned against false teachers. Speaking to the Galatians, he said at Gal. 1:6-9:

> *"I am astonished that you are so quickly deserting the one who called you to live in the grace of Christ and are turning to a different gospel which is really no gospel at all. Evidently some people are throwing you into confusion and are trying to pervert the gospel of Christ. But even if we or an angel from heaven should preach a gospel other than the one we preached to you, let them be under God's curse! As we have already said, so now I say again: If anybody is preaching to you a gospel other than what you accepted, let them be under God's curse!"*

I was deeply struck by these verses. It sounded familiar, like Paul was talking to me. It sounded like what God had just saved me from. A curse! A yoke of slavery!

So, what is the gospel? On an earlier mission, Paul said in Acts 20:24 that his only focus was to:

> *"...finish the race and complete the task the Lord Jesus has given me—the task of testifying to the good news of God's grace."*

Wow! This is an amazing revelation to me. Was it really that simple? The gospel of grace! But Paul wasn't finished with the Galatians yet. He continues in Galatians 3:1:

"You foolish Galatians! Who has bewitched you? Before your very eyes Jesus Christ was clearly portrayed as crucified."

The New World Translation of this same verse translates it this way: "...Who has brought you under this evil influence..." An excellent translation and again, it sounded like what I had just been released from.

Paul continues to teach the difference between grace and law through Galatians 3:10-13:

"For all who rely on the works of the law are under a curse, as it is written: 'Cursed is everyone who does not continue to do everything written in the Book of the Law.' Clearly no one who relies on the law is justified before God, because 'the righteous will live by faith.' The law is not based on faith; on the contrary, it says, 'The person who does these things will live by them.' Christ redeemed us from the curse of the law by becoming a curse for us, for it is written: 'Cursed is everyone who is hung on a pole.'"

And Gal. 5:1:

"It is for freedom that Christ has set us free. Stand firm, then, and do not let yourselves be burdened again by a yoke of slavery."

All these passages are eye-opening. I AM FREE! YOU ARE FREE! WE ARE ALL FREE! Free from carrying the weight and burden of our sins. For so long I had been living under the law, oblivious to God's grace and its abundant blessings.

Still, some will erroneously assume that with grace we have the freedom to do whatever we want without any restraint; that grace gives one a license to sin. True to human nature, that is precisely what the Romans believed.

In Romans 6:15 Paul was asked:

> *"What then? Shall we sin because we are not under the law but under grace? By no means!"*

Grace, indeed, has the opposite effect. In Galatians 3:19, it asks:

> *"Why, then, was the law given at all? It was added because of transgressions until the Seed to whom the promise referred had come. The law was given through angels and entrusted to a mediator."*

The day I started learning about God's grace and grasping its full meaning is the day the mental chains started falling off. I realized I had been living under the law covenant and trying to "work" for my salvation. Ephesians 2:8, 9 says this about "works:"

> *"For it is by grace you have been saved, through faith— and this is not from yourselves, it is the gift of God— not by works, so that no one can boast."*

Not to justify my behavior or anything, but it was all becoming clearer to me now. In the past, going before the brothers never gave me a sense of relief or forgiveness. It left me with feelings of worthlessness. The decision of the elders—whether it be private reproof, public reproof, or disfellowshipping—was a representation of God's mercy toward me. Law and confessing to men perpetuate a pattern or cycle of sin. Jesus' sacrifice broke that cycle. Accepting God's forgiveness was something I was not capable of in the past. Instead, I would wonder how Jehovah could ever forgive a sinner like me. This is what law does! It condemns you. It is rigid, but love and grace are flexible.

The problem with the law is that we cannot live up to it. Paul teaches us that we cannot live under both grace and law; we must choose one or the other. If we choose to live under the law, then we must live by it completely and suffer the consequences by it. Or we can simply choose to live under grace.

I choose grace.

Love under the law, the old law covenant, the mosaic law covenant is conditional. It is dependent on a set of circumstances. Since grace, the new law covenant, is love, that love is unconditional and not dependent on anything we do or don't do.

And what better way to experience grace than through baptism in the name of Jesus.

With each layer of deception that I uncovered and my awakening to the truth; I began to wonder if my baptism thirty-five years ago was valid. After all, I was baptized into an organization. As a fifty-year-old, I didn't want to make that mistake again.

With where I was at in my journey, I wondered:

- Should I get baptized again?
- What was different about baptism in a church?

- Since I accepted Jesus as my Lord and Savior, did I really need to be baptized by water?

The first time I was baptized there were some things I had to do in order to be considered ready. This included studying two books, which took about six months each to complete. After making a personal dedication to Jehovah in prayer, I expressed an interest in baptism. Arrangements were made to answer eighty questions in front of an elder. The entire process could take up to two years. Depending on how you answered, the elders would decide if you were ready for baptism or not. My answers to the eighty questions were acceptable and I was considered ready for baptism. It was an exciting time!

On the day of baptism, all the candidates sat in the front row of an assembly or convention and there were two questions asked in front of the crowd. One of the questions asked is if "you understand that your baptism identifies you as one of Jehovah's Witnesses in association with" his organization. Then the speaker would say: "Your answer please." All the candidates responded simultaneously: "YES!"

I felt a desire to be baptized in the name of the Father, Son, and Holy Spirit, and I decided I would participate in this sacred experience with my new church.

It was going to take some time, though. This time I would ask the questions because I would not allow myself to get fooled again.

After one of the services, I went up to one of the pastors, Barry, and told him I was interested in getting baptized. But only after I got satisfactory answers to my questions. I pulled out my list of questions (yes, I had a list). This is what I asked:

- Who owns this church?
- How is it structured?
- What books do I need to study?
- How do you handle wrongdoing?
- Do you disfellowship people?
- What if I decide I don't want to go to this church anymore, are you going to stop talking to me?
- If I write a book, do I have to get permission from you?
- Do I have to get permission to start a YouTube channel?

Barry listened intently as I began to bombard him with questions, one after the other. He seemed perplexed but graciously allowed me to finish. Then he began to answer every single question as his wife, Eva, sat in the background, waiting patiently.

I did not have the chance to finish asking all my questions, as he took over speaking and answered every single question including the other questions I never got to. It was as if the Holy Spirit took over and was speaking through him. His answers put me at ease, and I felt a wave of peace come over me.

At times I suspected his thoughts were along these lines: You poor child. What happened to you over there? However, as these questions flowed from me and the answers flowed from him, I realized I had freedom in Christ. He said something about me being free to make my own decisions.

Just nothing bizarre, I guess, like starting a church or a religion. No, that was not of interest to me. Making sure I was not getting trapped and I had options was most important to me. While I may not have had all the answers and I hadn't finished reading the Bible, as I promised myself I would, I had "an out" if I needed it or if anything went left.

I thanked Barry for his time, went home, and prayed about it. Three days passed and I couldn't think of any more questions or anything that prevented me from getting baptized. I knew I was ready.

I chose the date of January 12, 2019, as my baptism day.

I was filled with excitement and nervousness the entire day. I spent the entire day with God, meditating, reading my Bible and praying. I knew I was doing the right thing and it felt like this step made the adoption complete, as if God had adopted me officially.

At this time, I had not started reading the New Testament in the Bible yet. When I got to Romans 9:26 which says: *"In the very place where it was said to them, 'You are not my people,' there they will be called 'children of the living God,'"* I had a flashback to the announcement that was made that I was no longer one of Jehovah's Witnesses and the feeling of acceptance and "reinstatement" I had this special day.

As we walked down to the baptism area, I asked Barry if he had any questions for me. He looked at me with a calming smile and said: "Nope, no questions."

I was getting baptized on my word! The personal declaration I made in prayer and simply letting them know I was ready was enough.

The day symbolized a fresh new start, a well-deserved and desperately needed one.

I thought only my daughter would be there. But when I got to the baptism area, the ladies from my Bible study group "Gracetime," were there too. Susan was there, in the background as well, which meant a lot. She attended the same church and I had always tried to avoid her so she wouldn't think I was stalking her and to make sure I was not crossing our professional boundaries.

Outside, in the baptismal fountain, I stood in the water, waiting. The baptism would also be broadcast in the auditorium. I was overjoyed and anxious at the same time.

I was struggling to keep my emotions in check, all the while with a smile on my face. I was thinking, *dunk me now before I burst into tears.* Finally, Barry began to speak: "We baptize these, Gail Theresa White, in the name of the Father, Son, and Holy Spirit. Buried to death unto Christ, (I was dipped) raised to walk in the newness of life."

Raised to walk in the newness of life. It was such an overwhelming and beautiful experience of acceptance, not by a religion or by a church, but by God. I felt brand new, redeemed and it was magnificent. It still brings tears to my eyes when I think about that day and when I see others give their life to Christ and get baptized. I am forever in awe of this powerful moment.

It's quite simple. Grace is a gift, free of charge; a gift we don't have to work for and a gift we cannot repay. There is no amount of works one can do to earn salvation. Salvation is not earned on our goodness or because of what I do, but because of what Jesus did.

When I learned I was no longer under the law but under grace, my whole world became bright. My relationship with God and Jesus was not dependent upon the standards of Watchtower and what the elders in the community deemed me worthy of; it was what God deemed me worthy of that mattered most.

The day I stopped working for my salvation, was the day I got free and started living. A boulder had been lifted off my chest and I could breathe again. In my mind, I thought I was walking away and giving up on trying to live the Christian life. I had messed up so badly that Jehovah didn't want me in his organization. Somehow, I had become a perfectionist who was trying to make up for everything I had done wrong; thinking I could work it off. I just couldn't do it anymore and I was exhausted from working so hard.

Jesus died for me and his death set me free from the condemnation of my sins. The work is already finished. All that is required is that I believe in him and have faith.

*"...Believe in the Lord Jesus, and you will be saved—
you and your household."*

Acts 16:31

It is as simple as it sounds.

Realizing the blood of Jesus covered my sins has helped me
to share my story without shame.

Today, I have forgiven myself and I accept God's
forgiveness. I no longer question it.

Today, I am free from the burden of my sin and I am
confident that He no longer holds my sins against me. I no
longer associate life's struggle with God's disapproval of me
or see it as punishment for some unforgiven act.

I choose to live under grace, and this choice has made all the
difference in the past year. Accepting God's grace not only
helped me learn to forgive myself, but it also taught me how
to forgive those who hurt me, whether they are aware of it or
not, as well as those who never apologized or never will.

God's grace taught me that I am enough, just the way I am,
and I see myself the way He sees me.

Grace exonerated me.

10 | IT WAS A SET-UP. NOW I'M SET UP!

"It was good for me to be afflicted so that I might learn your decrees."

Psalm 119:71

Trying to live in two worlds—one which demands you be a good witness and manage all the expectations that go along with it; the other, the real world in which you must function, even when it is no longer feasible. These were my two worlds and they collided; neither part of my existence compatible with the other.

If you're wondering how I didn't lose my mind, believe me, I've wondered the same thing myself. But I didn't, and this is my testimony to the goodness of God.

If I had only been reproved, I would have gone back into the routine as a JW. Worse yet, I would have never come to know Christ and have an intimate relationship with Him.

Isolation was needed to restructure my entire world. It helped me see exactly where I needed to be. The ones who put me there were not counting on this, but God was. It turns out, I was too.

I learned a lot in isolation. Through isolation, God can work wonders in our lives. It's where He does His best work and where we learn to trust Him. He heals us and shows us how to look to Him for all the power we need. He was not punishing me; rather, he removed toxic people out of my life and removed me from toxic situations that were destroying me. He was protecting me for a season, and He's not done with me yet. I am still a work in progress.

But I do know this, if you start to see people or situations breaking off and falling out of your life, let it happen.

The scales fell off my eyes that September night when they handed down the verdict to disfellowship me. That's what the flash of light I sensed was. And I thank God.

I was looking to men for forgiveness and acceptance, not realizing I had it all along. Completely overlooking the fact that 1 Tim. 2:5 says: *"For there is one God and one mediator between God and mankind, the man Christ Jesus, who gave himself as a ransom for all people."* The loving arrangement God set up for the forgiveness of my sins was nailed to a tree over 2,000 years ago.

But that is no excuse for the harmful actions of men, especially those who claim to be His representatives.

What they meant for evil, God overturned it and opened my eyes to the truth. Once the noise around me was silenced I could identify with Joseph when he said at Gen. 50:20 that *"...God intended it for good."*

In the early days, if I ran into a witness who said hello to me because they didn't know I was disfellowshipped, it was expected that I would tell them. I no longer do that because I am not one of Jehovah's Witnesses and I no longer live by their mandates. Today, I am free, and I have redemption. I am fully liberated to live an authentic life, with a one world view.

No longer do I wear the label "disfellowshipped" that was designed to keep me in bondage, to make me feel rejected and to make me feel like an outcast. The way to get that label lifted is to go back. No longer do I refer to myself as an outsider, the way one is made to feel when they are ousted from the congregation. But by the grace of God, I have been able to reject that man-made label. If someone asks me if I am reinstated, my answer is yes.

The only label I respond to now is that I am a child of the living God and so are all of you who believe.

I have joined in with the one and only King Jesus and the Body of Christ.

Of course, by the time word gets around that I am not returning, I will be accused of being an apostate, or that I want to continue living my life of sin, or of having an independent spirit like Eve, someone who wants to make their own decisions independent of God. These attempts to hold me down cannot work any longer because I have freedom in Christ.

Watchtower portrays through videos anyone who leaves the organization as being strung out on drugs and alcohol, clubbing and living a sexual immoral lifestyle. They don't talk about those who are living clean lives. In fact, they believe it's not possible to live a morally clean life without the organization.

What makes this choice heartbreaking is that parents have gone to their graves never reconciling with their children, never meeting their grandchildren. How sad and not of God! I am not the first and I won't be the last. This is how it is and could be my reality one day. Sure, I can go back, get reinstated and all will be well again. But then, their emotional blackmail would have worked. After what I have learned so far, I am no longer willing to justify it.

I thank God every day for getting me out of that organization. In hindsight, it had to happen this way. It is the best thing that could have ever happened. Through the process I learned to forgive myself, accept myself and love myself mistakes and all.

Had I remained in the organization, I would have lived a life where I cherry-picked what I wanted to believe. In my new life I cannot do this. While my belief system is still developing, I have begun to rebuild it and my faith is stronger than it has ever been.

If you find yourself in a similar position, you may be asking yourself a series of questions.

- Why me?
- How could I have been so deceived?
- Why didn't I see this before?
- Why did I go through all this?
- What is it all for?
- What is my role?
- Is there something I should be doing about it?

Know that you are not alone. Don't suffer in silence. Things may seem silent in your life, like nothing is moving, but God is working behind the scenes.

As painful as the transition is, it is a necessary part of the healing process. Take the time to grieve and reevaluate what may have been a lifetime of teachings and indoctrination. Be patient and loving with yourself, because as you heal and learn about God's Holy Truth, you will be able to replace intense and volatile emotions with love, ideas, and emotions which build a foundation to help you grow toward Jesus directly, not through any other channel.

If these words speak to you as someone who has been a witness, try these things:

Accept God's forgiveness. Take Him at his Word. If you repent and believe, your sins are forgiven. He does not bring up your past and He does not remember your sins. Accept that Jesus died for you and God cares for you as an individual. The bible says, He removes our sins as far as the east is from the west and makes our sins white as snow, as if it never happened. What a peaceful thought!

Forgive yourself. After you accept God's forgiveness, the next step in your healing process is to forgive yourself. You have much to learn and you may be relearning a new life and a new way of thinking with completely different boundaries and rules. It would be great to get an instant reboot; however, there is great beauty in the journey of self-discovery. Savor this!

Do not be angry and disappointed with yourself for falling for this deception. Instead, take courage because this deception was prophesied in the Bible, all throughout the New Testament. In many of the epistles of Paul, false prophets are spoken of—the wolves in sheep's clothing.

Seek out a therapist. Healing is possible and you are in full control. But you may find that a little extra help is needed.

171

This is where therapy can play a huge role in your recovery. So many stigmas lie with the valuable guidance that comes from seeing a therapist. Trained therapists create a safe environment where you can vent your truths, regardless of what they may be. Additionally, confidentiality is part of a therapist's code of ethics. There are exceptions to this, especially when a child may be in danger, sexually or physically. In return, you can work with someone who is equipped to not inject their own indoctrination, but to listen and help guide you to resolutions which can bring peace to heart and mind.

Take care of yourself, spiritually and physically! As you make significant life changes, such as leaving an organization you thought was the truth and seeking out what is the truth, it can take a toll on you in various ways. Learn to be kind to yourself and acknowledge that what you went through was not normal. A transition such as this is a very traumatic experience. You will be blessed with good days and struggle through the challenges of bad days too. Taking care of yourself is what you must do in order to remain strong; to build your resilience.

Understand there is a purpose to your pain. Free yourself from shame, guilt, and condemnation. Stop beating yourself up for things in your past and things you have no control over. Realize Jesus can give you a fresh start. There is no condemnation in Christ, and we become new creatures when we believe in Him. No label can take this away from you.

The answer as to why I had to endure what I did, is no longer relevant. But it is my obligation and driving force to understand all of this, collect the information and learn to relay it so I can make a difference for someone who knows something is not quite right and desires a change. A better fight has begun.

Do I still get upset about wasted years and mistreatment? Absolutely! It is an emotional and traumatic experience to realize your belief was misaligned; that the best years of your life have been wasted. While I hope I have many years left, I cannot help but think of those who lost their lives out of despair; the ones who could not hold on any longer.

People sometimes ask how I could walk away. This is a fair question; one anyone currently in the Watchtower organization would understand better than most how difficult this decision is. They ask if I ever see myself going back, or they make a comment on how strong I have been.

I have my moments, but those questions make me wonder if I've become just as hard-hearted as those witnesses who are shunning me. In my mind, once I saw through the deception, choosing to follow Jesus came naturally. If I'm being honest, it's not an easy thing to live without your family. It's unnatural really. Yet God has protected my heart, taken off the coat of heaviness and replaced it with peace.

Here are a few more lessons I learned along my journey:

If you feel like crying, cry. Releasing emotions and anxieties is a big part of this process. Maybe you're like me and don't like crying in public (who does?). If you have an emotion that needs to be released, don't stuff it or try to hold it in. It is a kind thing to do for yourself to release it. A good cry is like a shower for your soul.

If you are tired, sleep. Even Jesus rested. Only people who have been through the experience we've been through as a JW really understand the toll it takes on the mind and body. God knows and He is watching over you. A little extra sleep may be needed through this transition.

Be intentional about what you put into your body. Commit to your health because you have many exciting new things coming your way! Letting go of the burden of trying to achieve an unachievable standard, along with healthy eating and exercise, helped me to lose 43 pounds.

Be intentional about what you put into your heart and mind. Listen to upbuilding music; read inspiring books; grant yourself permission to walk away from toxic people and situations. Stay clear of what drowns out God's Word and tries to trump it with man-made rules. Once you realized what has happened to you, be smart and inquisitive to ensure it does not happen again. I've learned that God's greatest advocates are not perfect individuals. He can turn your trials into a testament of his goodness.

Embrace your spiritual journey at whatever point you are at. Your spiritual journey is intimate, more so than most anything else you can experience in life. Upon reflection, when I was asked where I was at spiritually, it should have set off red flags. What began with an inquiry about my relationship with God grew into man judging me to see if I was "spiritual enough." Spirituality does not come from the things we do or don't do. No other human can or should judge your relationship with God.

Appreciate the place isolation has brought you to. It can be very trying at first, but only through isolation can you begin to separate yourself from what is most threatening to you. I learned it wasn't God out to get me, it was the devil who was trying to keep me away from God's plan for my life. Knowing this opened me up to the healing process. God can heal your broken heart and make you whole again, if you let Him in.

Today, my circle of family and friends may be small, but they are mighty and the real deal. The love is unconditional. They don't judge me and I'm free to be myself. Don't we all desire this?

Dumbing myself down to fit in, accurately described me for a long while. Honestly, things never added up, but I didn't allow myself to dwell on it. I recall asking my dad one time, when we studied as a family: "Is Jehovah really going to destroy everyone who is not a Jehovah's Witness? What about people who have never heard of Him?" Even though I was about six years old at the time, it didn't seem fair to me.

They used God's Word to alienate me and others to get us to conform by using acts of separation against us. This organization can look good on the surface, but there is an underlying cruelty to it that cannot possibly originate from a God of love who wants all His children to be loved and grow toward know Him.

All I've come to learn so far is because I had a desire to understand the Bible, the true Word of God, not a grossly mistranslated version—a version used to discipline and correct me. If the Bible is a two-edged sword, able to pierce hearts, used for disciplining and reproving in righteousness, JW's are using the equivalent of a butter knife.

I have great empathy for struggling witnesses and those who know (or know of) these individuals. It compels me to act, to write this very account of my life. To those who see this unfolding in another's life, know this: Someone who is caught into the stronghold of the Watchtower organization is fearful of what happens if they leave. After all, they will be forced to leave so much behind. That has not changed for a long time and all indications are that the organization is doubling down on this man-made policy.

So, to the best of your ability, continue to show love and acceptance. Be kind and patient. You'd be amazed at how far basic human decency can go. If you know God and love Him, you realize the power of accepting people where they are on their journey toward Him.

Unfortunately, genuine love and compassion you show may be taken apprehensively—an alarm for ill intentions. Genuine love feels foreign, which makes this leeriness feel right.

Be mindful that you may not be able to wake up a JW. Any persuasive reasoning may be perceived as an attack on their spirituality and they will think you are trying to mislead them. JWs are taught that non-JWs are bad and wicked. Direct attacks only strengthen their programming and strengthens their resolve to remain loyal no matter what. You can, however, plant seeds that get them to think.

And, please, do not feel offended if they do not warm up to you right away. Many have been so hurt and disillusioned by the reality of this organization that they have become agnostic or atheist, not wanting to have anything to do with religion. I totally understand how this is possible. Can you blame them? Some have spiraled into a debilitating depression and experience the complications of this state-of-mind. Their main question: How could a loving God allow certain things to happen and why hasn't he done anything about it yet?

Still, we do not judge. By understanding the constraints which JWs have likely grown up in, or into, you can only imagine a noose around someone's neck being slowly tightened to the point of suffocation, only happening so slowly it is unrecognizable at first. Having a non-judgmental, non-invasive approach could mean everything at some point.

You may feel you need to understand all the JW teachings to help someone. This is untrue; the true Word of God is omnipotent and all-powerful, compared to the teachings of the Watchtower Bible and Tract Society.

Despite giving fifty years of my life to a lie, I could either let it keep me stuck or allow it to propel me. I chose to use it as a springboard to bring awareness to what really goes on behind closed doors.

God is truly near to the brokenhearted. He was there when no one else was in my life; at least not the people who I believed would be.

He kept his word. He had me and held onto me the entire time, never letting me go. I never lost His favor and He never abandoned me. Through the clearer lens of faith and understanding, I now see that nothing was random. I was never alone and now I am in a place of culmination.

It was a set up that lead me to be the happiest I have ever been. How can that be since my life as I knew it longer exists? Family, friends, becoming an empty nester, the business I loved, even my faith, all went up in flames. Everything around me seemed to be a loss and figuratively burned to the ground becoming ashes. But I am rebuilding, stronger with God this time. He promised that He can make beauty out of ashes and He will get the glory.

He healed me and made me whole again. I am not a victim; I am a victor and I am no longer lost. I learned the truth about Jesus and found redemption, forgiveness, compassion, and grace that only comes through Him.

I encourage you to do your own research, examine the Bible for yourself, and become your own Expert Witness.

I found a new beginning and now I am set up on God's plan; a plan of grace and love.

179

"For if you remain silent at this time, relief and deliverance for the Jews will arise from another place, but you and your father's family will perish. And who knows but that you have come to your royal position for such a time as this."

Esther 4:14

EXPERT WITNESS FINAL REPORT

APPENDIX A | ADDITIONAL REFERENCES

These excerpts are further evidence of how Watchtower delivers the message to JW's, trusting in blind belief.

Keep Yourself in God's Love, "How to Treat a Disfellowshipped Person." Appendix, pp. 207-208.

Is strict avoidance really necessary?

Yes, for several reasons. First, it is a matter of loyalty to God and his Word. We obey Jehovah not only when it is convenient but also when doing so presents real challenges. Love for God moves us to obey all his commandments, recognizing that he is just and loving and that his laws promote the greatest good. (Isaiah 48:17; 1 John 5:3) Second, withdrawing from an unrepentant wrongdoer protects us and the rest of the congregation from spiritual and moral contamination and upholds the congregation's good name. (1 Corinthians 5:6, 7) Third, our firm stand for Bible principles may even benefit the disfellowshipped one. By supporting the decision of the judicial committee, we may touch the heart of a wrongdoer who thus far has failed to respond to the efforts of the elders to assist him. Losing precious fellowship with loved ones may help him to come "to his senses," see the seriousness of his wrong, and take steps to return to Jehovah.—Luke 15:17.

Watchtower, September 25, 1951, Page 25, says: "A simple hello to someone can be the first step that develops into a conversation and maybe even a friendship."

Watchtower, "Are you remaining clean in every respect?" Subheading: "Keeping on Guard" to Stay Morally Clean. November 1, 1987, paragraph 10.

10. (a) What is one reason so many are reproved or disfellowshipped each year? (b) What Bible principle should guide our conduct on vacations and at work?

[10] At Ephesians 5:5 Paul warned: "For you know this, recognizing it for yourselves, that no fornicator or unclean person or greedy person—which means being an idolater—has any inheritance in the kingdom of the Christ and of God." Yet, thousands each year are reproved or disfellowshipped because of sexual immorality—'sinning against the body.' (1 Corinthians 6:18) Often, it is simply a result of not "keeping on guard according to [God's] word." (Psalm 119:9) Many brothers, for example, drop their moral guard during vacation periods. Neglecting theocratic association, they strike up friendships with worldly vacationers. Reasoning that these are 'really nice people,' some Christians have joined them in questionable activities. Similarly, others have become overly friendly with their workmates. One Christian elder became so involved with a female employee that he abandoned his family and took up living with her! Disfellowshipping resulted. How true the

Bible's words, "Bad associations spoil useful habits"!—1 Corinthians 15:33.

Watchtower, "Always Accept Jehovah's Discipline" November 15, 2006, paragraphs 12-13.

12, 13. What can result from trying to hide wrongdoing?

12 If you have committed a serious sin, confession can help you to regain a good conscience. (1 Timothy 1:18-20) But failure to confess could result in a defiled conscience that could lead you into more sin. Remember that your sin is not just against another human or the congregation. It is against God. The psalmist sang: "Jehovah—in the heavens is his throne. His own eyes behold, his own beaming eyes examine the sons of men. Jehovah himself examines the righteous one as well as the wicked one."—Psalm 11:4, 5.

13 Jehovah will not bless anyone who hides gross sin and tries to stay in the clean Christian congregation. (James 4:6) So if you have fallen into sin and want to do what is right, do not hesitate to make an honest confession. Otherwise, you will have a guilty conscience, especially when you read or hear counsel regarding such serious matters. What if Jehovah were to withdraw his spirit from you, as he did in the case of King Saul? (1 Samuel 16:14) With God's spirit removed, you could fall into even more serious sin.

19. When do we need to stop associating with someone in the congregation?

¹⁹ In a loving family, each member does his part to make the others happy. But imagine that one person rebels. Everybody in the family tries again and again to help him, but he rejects the help. He may decide to leave home, or the head of the family may have to ask him to leave. Something similar can happen in the congregation. A person may choose to keep doing things that displease Jehovah and harm the congregation. He rejects help and shows by his actions that he no longer wants to be part of the congregation. He may choose to leave the congregation himself, or he may have to be disfellowshipped. If this happens, the Bible clearly says that we should "stop keeping company" with him. (Read 1 Corinthians 5:11-13; 2 John 9-11) This can be very difficult if he is a friend of ours or a member of our family. But in a situation like this, our loyalty to Jehovah must be stronger than our loyalty to anyone else.—See Endnote 8.

20, 21. (a) How does the disfellowshipping arrangement show love? (b) Why is it important that we choose our friends wisely?

²⁰ The disfellowshipping arrangement is a loving provision from Jehovah. It keeps the congregation safe from those who do not care about Jehovah's standards. (1 Corinthians 5:7; Hebrews 12:15, 16) It helps us to show love for Jehovah's holy name, for his high standards, and for Jehovah

himself. (1 Peter 1:15, 16) And the disfellowshipping arrangement shows love for the person who is no longer a member of the congregation. This strong discipline may help him to realize that what he is doing is wrong and motivate him to change. Many who were once disfellowshipped later returned to Jehovah and were warmly welcomed back into the congregation.—Hebrews 12:11.

²¹ In one way or another, our friends affect us. So it is important that we choose them carefully. If we love those whom Jehovah loves, we will be surrounded by people who can help us to stay faithful to him forever.

Endnote 8: Disfellowshipping

When someone who has seriously sinned does not repent and refuses to follow Jehovah's standards, he can no longer be a member of the congregation. He needs to be disfellowshipped. When someone is disfellowshipped, we have no more dealings with that person and we stop talking to him. (1 Corinthians 5:11; 2 John 9-11) The disfellowshipping arrangement protects Jehovah's name and the congregation. (1 Corinthians 5:6) Disfellowshipping is also discipline that can help someone to repent so that he can return to Jehovah.—Luke 15:17.

GOD'S HANDIWORK IN "SMALL" THINGS

Not every story found a place in the main content of this book, but I would be remiss to not mention how God works in incredible ways, not only large but small too. Recognizing this has helped greatly in my journey toward truth and a true understanding of God's nature.

The car I spoke about earlier, had a defect. The brake pump in it would fail and this meant you could not stop the car when it did. Replacing this with the warranty—no problem. Realizing it must be replaced about eight years after the warranty, now that was a problem. It was no cheap repair, a few thousand dollars minimal.

After one such episode in May 2017, I found myself at the dealership, upset and trying to figure out how to handle this issue. "Do you think this is right?" I asked. "I couldn't stop the car. How can this be acceptable?"

They explained it was one of those maintenance parts that needed replacement every now and again, like new tires.

I emphatically disagreed.

We started battling about this and I just left my car there. My attorney wrote a letter to the dealership and the manufacturer.

A couple months passed by and they called me up and asked what I was going to do with the car. My answer was simple: "You got the letter from my attorney. Do what it says and then I will come and get the car when it's ready."

I did need it fixed, too. It's not like I had an extra vehicle around. It had taken lots of shuffling to manage everything during this time. We were at a standstill, the dealership refused to fix my car and threatened to have it towed.

Eventually, I caved in paid for the $2,400 repair in November 2017. As I paid this I thought, *here it goes. Up until this point, there had been so much loss already, now my car?* I guess I really did lose Jehovah's favor. *What's next, God, my house?*

Leaving in my car that day, my three nephews were with me. Ten miles down the road, the brakes failed on me again. I could not stop the car and had it towed back to the dealership. This time the alternator and battery went out. How suspicious...right when a brand-new pump was replaced.

This was when I put my fighting gloves on and contacted every regulatory agency I could think of including the NHTSA. It didn't matter that the manufacturer was an international giant.

I felt utterly defeated. A whole year passed by.

In August 2018, I finally received a letter from the manufacturer. It was good news; really good news. The warranty for the brake pump had been extended to twenty-five years. Who has ever heard of such a thing? In addition, whatever money I spent on repairs would be refunded to me.

I was in disbelief. I was getting my money back and the manufacturer finally took responsibility for the defect. Realizing what a big win this was, I dropped to my knees and thanked God. Again, another win for me when I was supposed to be going through a period where everything should be going wrong.

The yearlong battle was over. In the end, I had made my grievance known in the natural and God took over in the supernatural. I had put it out of my mind and counted it as a loss. It may have been easier for me to just sell the car during this time. Someone would have been eager to get it for a good price. However, integrity does matter, and mine would not allow me to sell the car knowing the defect it had. But He had been working on it the entire time and had given me the victory.

God has shown me over the years that He does care about the desires of the heart, even the material things. All of it had God's touch on it in one way or the other.

It felt like God was saying to me: *Any more questions?* Nothing is impossible for Him and from this point on, I no longer questioned if I had his favor or not.

Learning More About Jesus

Christmas Eve Candlelight Service

Before I was baptized, I decided to go to the Christmas Eve candlelight service. I'd never gotten to experience anything regarding this night. I had no idea what to expect, but the experience quickly revealed a great deal to me.

It became a turning point and it was so emotionally compelling.

Praising and worshipping Jesus, giving Him honor and appreciating the significance of His birth and how miraculous it was.

The beautiful connection to God and the birth of His son was everywhere in the room that beautiful night. It was so much to take in and then the speaker asked if anyone was ready to give their lives to Jesus and accept Him as their Lord and Savior. If yes, please come forward.

Last time I was at a service and this was asked, I did not get up.

This time, I did not rule it out.

Five minutes passed by.

It was silent and the lights dim.

As I reconciled my intense feelings, I realized a sense of gratitude for being in that moment. It was a perfect time. I finally got up and made my way down the aisle.

Once there, the pastor had no idea how to react to me. I was so emotional; all he could do was pat me on the back. My tears were filled with so much gratitude and uncontrollable emotion from this intimate connection with Jesus. I had found Jesus… No, wait, Jesus had found me!

Jesus led me in the right direction. He left the ninety-nine and came for me, and for this, I am forever grateful.

After four months, I finally filled out the visitor's card and it felt like home, like I had finally come home.

When I left the building that night, I sat in my car and just cried.

Why would a religion do what JWs had done to Jesus? How could they?

How could they obscure His identity and mislead so many people?

I was heartbroken that I never gave Jesus the honor, praise, and worship He deserved. He had done so much for me. Fifty years into my life, I have never been filled with such gratitude.

The story of Job's struggles had always intrigued me. I could relate and the trials he endured resonated with me. People accusing him of wrongdoing, of concealing a sin, misjudging him, all the loss. Useless comforters, I believe is how it is expressed.

This is how I have felt about the elders for so long. They offer no comfort and only add to one's burden.

In reading the account of Job, I never understood what he was repenting for when he said: "My ears had heard of you but now my eyes have seen you. Therefore, I despise myself and repent in dust and ashes (Job 42:5, 6)."

I have read Job's story about twenty times in my life, each time wondering what he was repenting for. If in the first chapter it called Job a blameless man, why did he need to repent?

That Christmas Eve night I found my answer. All my life I had heard of God, but that night I saw him. He came to life and He was pointing me in the right direction. I repented for not having seen Him before.

My entire life was now viewed from a whole new light.

Good Friday and Resurrection Sunday

In April 2019, I attended my first Good Friday service at Second Baptist Church. When I walked in there was a sea of people waiting in the lobby, most wearing black. My anxiety was on the rise a bit because I had no idea what to expect. I felt awkward because I was not properly dressed for the occasion.

This service seemed to be equivalent to the Lord's Evening Meal, the annual memorial of Jesus' death the witnesses celebrated once a year.

Walking into the auditorium I was greeted with silence. There was a message on the screen that said: "Please enter with reverence and silence." This was an immediate contrast between what I had known and what I was now learning.

There was no happy chatter anywhere; it was not a happy occasion.

The service felt like a real memorial. We were asked to kneel and pray. My daughter was with me and we held hands as we did. I felt her tears dropping on my hands, just as mine were dropping on hers. We were so overcome with emotion. Never had we experienced such a profound reverence being given to Jesus.

In addition, we partook of the communion. Something we had never done at the kingdom hall. That participation was reserved for those of the anointed class, the 144,000. In previous years, I just passed the plate down the line. Looking back now, it's as if I was saying *no thanks* to Jesus. That was such a moving experience for me.

After the service, I learned there was a Sunday service to celebrate the Resurrection of Jesus. I was surprised by this and asked someone which service had more significance, Good Friday or Resurrection Sunday? The gentleman indicated that this was a common question that has been discussed extensively. Jesus had to die for our sins but if He were never resurrected…

I concluded that there was nothing wrong with celebrating both. The heaviness of Jesus' crucifixion and the happiness of His resurrection.

I was so convicted. Then to top it off, after the Good Friday Service, a tour with twelve booths was set up. Each one signified an event leading up to Jesus' death. The first station was the beautiful act of servitude when Jesus washed the feet of his disciples, and it took us on a journey all the way through the crucifixion, showing replicas of the items used that day, including the whip, the nails, a torn curtain, and a replica of the Ark of the Covenant; a reminder of how this is no longer needed because we now have direct access to God.

This moment highlighted the contradiction between JWs and the truth. I had direct access! Not through an elder or anyone claiming to have a self-appointed channel of communication with God. But directly.

The Sunday service was a more upbeat atmosphere and message. The story of how Jesus rose from the dead was shared and how He revealed himself to his disciples. In my life, I had yet to be so overwhelmed with the meaning behind all these holy events. Now I had an idea. It was gut-wrenching and emotional as I felt the Holy Spirit flowing through me.

By this time, I had gone an entire year with an abundance of first experiences, each refreshing to me in all ways. The cautious side of everything still exists and I verify everything. Like the Beroeans in the Apostle Paul's day, we're encouraged to examine the scriptures. I did and it fit; not through manipulation to a certain message but through God's written Word.

Amen.

OPEN LETTER TO WATCHTOWER

Guys, the jig is up. You have deceived people for 140 years and have purposely thrown innocent people into confusion by preaching a different gospel. As Paul said: "*...which is really no gospel at all*. (Galatians 1:6, 7 NIV)" But many are waking up to the deception.

You have controlled the lives of good-hearted people far too long by going beyond what is written in the scriptures and adding to their burdens. Your policies have broken up families, forever altered lives of children by covering up alleged sexual abuse and have driven people to suicide. The flock is weary and downtrodden. They are like sheep without a shepherd and you have made the Word of God invalid.

That loud buzzing sound you hear are all the Expert Witnesses banding together. We are like warriors in an army; locking arms and locking shields. We are advancing, breaking through the barrier and taking back what belongs to us. We have each other's back, we support each other, and we love each other unconditionally.

Your lies will continue to be exposed. The wheat has been separated from the weeds. The harvest is here. The reason so many are leaving is because God is calling out His people and they are listening. "My sheep listen to my voice; I know them, and they follow me. (John 10:27)" We are all God's children, not just a select few, *if* good graces fall upon you. The Lord has implored you to repent and you have refused. I sincerely hope you will do the right thing and choose God.

Those of us who are awake will continue to speak out about the abuses of Watchtower and the human rights violations, specifically, Articles 16 and 18 of the Universal Declaration of Human Rights. As you hide under the guise of religion and seek protection under the First Amendment of the Constitution of the United States of America, the freedom you exercise in the name of religion is not what our Founding Fathers had in mind. This is not freedom in Christ, which we are all entitled to.

Moving forward in the One True God's Name,

Gail Theresa White, Expert Witness

ABOUT GAIL THERESA WHITE

Gail White is a former 4th generation Jehovah's Witness. Through her experiences as a Jehovah's Witness, a religion whose parent company is called the Watchtower Bible and Tract Society, Inc., she has awoken to the harsh realities of this proclaimed religion.

Today, Gail brings awareness to the distinct differences between God's Word and the variations which exist through the Jehovah's Witnesses organization. Through her acclaimed book, Expert Witness, along with a soon-launching YouTube Channel, social media postings, and presentations and talks on the subjects, she has shed light on what happens within the organization best known for knocking on peoples' doors.

Made in the USA
Coppell, TX
01 December 2019

12227758R00118